Curriculum design for higher education is complex, challenging and can be profoundly rewarding. However, in the rush and tumble of teaching, evidence-based practice can take a backseat while teachers focus on just getting through. Cooper and Krishnan have written a practitioner's guide to unit (subject) design which provides reliable, pertinent advice for teachers and teaching teams. The authors bring many years of practical experience to the book which recognizes the normal rhythms and challenges of teaching in Australian universities. If you are looking for effective advice for Australian university teachers – here it is.

Professor Elizabeth Johnson PFHEA,
Deputy Vice-Chancellor Education, Deakin University

Higher education in Australia has advanced dramatically since the 1960s when I first graduated. This new publication by Sharon Cooper & Siva Krishnan challenges teachers to think outside the square (their own learning styles) when designing courses, creating learning experiences and devising relevant student assessment. The authors draw on examples from their university teaching careers to help new college and university teachers become more adept at offering students a satisfying and stimulating education. This "student-centred" approach, in courses and degrees framed by a generic higher education, should result in graduates being far better prepared for tackling professional and life experiences than I was.

Grahame Feletti, BSc, BAHons, PhD, *Retired Associate Professor of Higher Education, The University of Newcastle, Australia*

Effective Unit Design for Higher Education Courses

A clear and concise course design is integral to effective student learning in units of study; however, unit design can be a daunting task for academics. *Effective Unit Design for Higher Education Courses* is a practical resource based on theoretical foundations, designed to assist both professional course designers and academics with varied levels of curriculum design and development experience or background in higher education units and courses.

This book provides a variety of practical advice, skills and resources to assist academics in designing curriculum that focuses on enhancing student learning. Readers are given a range of evidence-based developmental tools that challenge some of the currently accepted conventions behind unit design. Appropriate for any skill level, this book is designed to provide an accessible and structured process to design or revitalise high-quality units of study. Chapters cover a range of topics including developing assessment methods, strategies for providing feedback and evaluating unit design. The book has been structured to follow a design process, but as unit design is non-linear, chapters can be read in any order depending on interest or need.

An essential guide for curriculum designers of all skill and experience levels, this book will appeal to all higher education academics tasked with an aspect of unit design.

Sharon A. Cooper was a mathematics teacher and lecturer in teacher education before becoming lecturer, Curriculum Design and Development at the University of Newcastle. In this role she has designed and coordinated Graduate Certificate units in course and assessment design. She now works as a sessional academic and curriculum design consultant.

Siva Krishnan is a senior lecturer in Engineering at Deakin University. His work as an engineer, and then engineering lecturer inspired his curriculum design and development work. He has provided leadership and support for many course improvement projects for Deakin Learning Futures. As Course Director, he oversees unit design and delivery with a particular focus on enriching students' learning experiences.

Effective Unit Design for Higher Education Courses
A Guide for Instructors

Sharon A. Cooper and Siva Krishnan

LONDON AND NEW YORK

First published 2020
by Routledge
2 Park Square, Milton Park, Abingdon, Oxon OX14 4RN

and by Routledge
52 Vanderbilt Avenue, New York, NY 10017

Routledge is an imprint of the Taylor & Francis Group, an informa business

© 2020 Sharon A. Cooper and Siva Krishnan

The right of Sharon A. Cooper and Siva Krishnan to be identified as authors of this work has been asserted by them in accordance with sections 77 and 78 of the Copyright, Designs and Patents Act 1988.

All rights reserved. No part of this book may be reprinted or reproduced or utilised in any form or by any electronic, mechanical, or other means, now known or hereafter invented, including photocopying and recording, or in any information storage or retrieval system, without permission in writing from the publishers.

Trademark notice: Product or corporate names may be trademarks or registered trademarks, and are used only for identification and explanation without intent to infringe.

British Library Cataloguing in Publication Data
A catalogue record for this book is available from the British Library

Library of Congress Cataloging-in-Publication Data
A catalog record has been requested for this book

ISBN: 978-0-367-24391-3 (hbk)
ISBN: 978-0-367-24390-6 (pbk)
ISBN: 978-0-429-28221-8 (ebk)

Typeset in Bembo
by Taylor & Francis Books

Contents

	List of illustrations	viii
	Preface	ix
1	Analysing the context for effective unit design	1
2	Designing unit learning outcomes	13
3	Developing assessment methods	28
4	Designing rubrics for enhancing student learning	40
5	Devising an overall strategy for providing feedback	52
6	Planning effective teaching and learning experiences and activities	64
7	Evaluating the design of your unit	83
	Appendix	92
	Index	103

Illustrations

Tables

1.1	Philosophical approaches to curriculum design	4
1.2	Situational analysis for designing units	5
1.3	Issues and perspectives on learning: applying theory to design practice	6
1.4	Developing the strategic rationale for a unit	9
2.1	Examples of ILOs pre- and post-revision	19
2.2	Action verbs for the cognitive processes dimension	22
2.3	Krathwohl's two-dimensional cognitive processes framework	23
2.4	SOLO Taxonomy verbs	24
2.5	Action verbs categories	25
3.1	Assessment methods for categories of ILOs	33
3.2	Purpose of assessment and challenges they present to stakeholders	36
4.1	The structure of a rubric	44
4.2	Too many standards	44
4.3	Fewer standards	44
4.4	Ideas for highest and next-to-highest standards	50
6.1	Higher education learning framework	65
6.2	Characteristics of deep vs surface learning	72
6.3	Documenting learning design	77
6.4	Characteristics of learning activities	79
7.1	Unit design evaluation criteria	84
7.2	Students as partners: partnership values and definition	86
A	Initial unit analysis	92
B	Checking ILOs	94
C	Planning ILOs	95
D	Evaluating assessment	96
E	Evaluating criteria and standards	98
F	Planning feedback	99
G	Planning unit evaluation	101

Preface

In an era of accreditation and student satisfaction ratings, pressure is being brought to bear upon academics to design "better" curriculum, teaching, learning and assessment more than ever before. Curriculum design, because of its theory-rich foundations, is not an easily developed expertise for those with little or no background in educational theory.

Few recent, Australian, publications exist. Biggs and Tang's *Teaching for Quality Learning at University* (2011) remains a staple for its common-sense arguments for constructive alignment; Toohey's *Designing Courses for Higher Education* (2008) also offers the reader a scholarly approach to designing units of study and degree courses, emphasising the impacts of ideologies on teaching and learning. These texts can be theory-heavy and can be off-putting for academics with limited experience in curriculum design. This is a shame from our perspective, because while the process of curriculum/unit design is challenging, it can be immensely creative and rewarding.

Academic staff in central teaching and learning units with specific curriculum and learning design expertise are usually called upon to assist discipline academics who may have limited educational experience or know-how in designing units and courses. Often, they are asked to consider how they will enable discipline academics to help students to demonstrate achievement of Intended Learning Outcomes (ILOs), and assess discipline-related and transferrable skills.

Our experience, as advisers for academics in design or redesign of units and courses, leads us to an understanding that they are in desperate need of an accessible "how to", or practical guide, that is based on sound theoretical foundations rather than a text which attempts to teach the theory of course design.

With this in mind, it is our hope that this book will equip those without an educational or teaching background, with the knowledge of curricular, pedagogical and assessment know-how that is neither "dumbed down" nor beyond grasp. We hope that this book is used by novices and experts alike to both establish and nurture a practical and positive perspective of unit design, unit evaluation, and unit redesign. For those who are interested in following a more scholarly pathway, we offer some useful readings. We hope it becomes a catalyst for talk about what might be.

x *Preface*

A profound challenge for academic advisers in supporting curriculum and learning design is to facilitate practical workshops to design units of study or degree courses in the context of the discipline rather than from a theoretical perspective. We have designed and conducted very successful unit as well as course design workshops based on, and as part of, our work in faculties and central teaching and learning units for a number of years. Through this, we have developed what we feel is a highly successful, practical, approach to designing units that academics have praised for its structure and support.

This guide provides not only sound practical advice to design units for higher education courses, gathered and synthesised from well-trusted sources, it also provides unit designers with a suite of evaluation and development tools that we developed over the years. We encourage unit designers to consider alternatives to traditional approaches and put the students' learning at the centre of their field of vision.

The tools provided in this guide challenge the sometimes taken-for-granted assumptions around designing units. It emphasises alignment to ensure engagement and lasting learning at the same time that it encourages innovation by targeting the complex learning needs of unit designers themselves.

Our purpose is that this book is not to be solely used as a way to address poor student satisfaction ratings, even though we know the catalyst for use may be just that. We know many unit designers, teachers and assessors may not see a need for unit revision if these are considered to be the sole arbiter of quality. We encourage everyone, regardless of how well a unit may be rated by internal student surveys, to take up the challenge and consider how student *learning* rather than student satisfaction can be enhanced by following the guidelines set out here.

The book has been divided into seven chapters, which can be read in any order depending on particular interest or needs. It is important to note that we have structured the book to follow a "design process", as indicated by the flow of chapters. The complexity of the unit design process can be difficult to grasp, and we do not want to imply that it is a simple linear process. For example, intended learning outcomes (Chapter 2) may be revised after considering assessment options (Chapter 3). A unit evaluation (Chapter 7) may precede a revision of feedback strategies (Chapter 5).

The first chapter looks at analysing the context of unit design. Until recently, units were often designed in isolation to the course or courses that they sit within. This practice is changing, but we are not fully there yet. A thorough analysis of the context of any unit is important to its success within a course. In this chapter, we take unit designers through a variety of approaches available to analyse the context and to help them develop a clear picture of the needs for designing a unit. Important to this step is attention to course-level thinking and ensuring a coherent course design. There may be other requirements at the course-level and therefore at the unit level including government and professional accreditation standards, graduate outcomes, work integrated learning, and learning certain academic skills. This chapter sets the scene for paying attention to the intent of the unit and planning student learning experiences and engagement.

In keeping with a now well-adopted outcomes-based approach, the second chapter will take the unit designers through a process of developing the ILOs that serve as the basis for sound constructive alignment (Biggs & Tang 2011). Like many, we use Bloom's Revised Taxonomy (Krathwohl 2002) to encourage a focus on low- to high-order thinking. We supplement this with Biggs's *SOLO Taxonomy* to guide unit designers to articulate the intended learning outcomes.

With *Assessment 2020: Seven propositions for assessment reform in higher education* (Boud & Associates 2010) in mind, the third chapter will focus on developing unit designers' approaches to assessment design, beginning with the analysis of alignment with ILOs. From here, analysing suitability (in terms of method, format, difficulty level and weighting), and considering other factors such as timing, diversity and clarity, will lead unit designers to the development of assessment tasks that work best for student engagement and success. A special first-year section will focus on informed good practice for assessing first-year students.

Chapter 4 asks unit designers to consider and articulate the quality of the work they require from students. Using a criterion-referenced / standards-based approach, unit designers will develop a set of criteria and standards that align with their outcomes and their tasks. A significant focus in this chapter is the development of rubric descriptors that inform students' work, provide grading validity and reliability, and serve as the basis for the provision of feedback to students.

An integrated, well-planned, strategy for the provision of feedback to students on both their graded and non-graded work is an essential unit performance measure. In Chapter 5, unit designers will explore a range of techniques and modes, which they can use to ensure feedback is effective and guides successful student engagement and learning.

In Chapter 6, unit designers can learn about a wide variety of learning activities that are most likely to develop deep learning in students. Informed by a variety of well-known educational theories and practice, we focus on choosing, sequencing and implementing activities that maximise students' learning. Particular attention is paid to the integrated development of students' academic skills/literacies.

The last chapter will focus on the development of a strategic approach to unit evaluation that provides a holistic, multifaceted combination of quantitative and qualitative data for determining the performance of your unit against the intentional design. Unit designers are shown how to select a range of strategies to consider at the design phase, ensuring that they are both targeted and integrated.

Finally, we provide additional evaluations and examples from across the disciplines to illustrate how our approach and process can be applied more generally.

This book starts from the premise that the role of the academic in higher education is quite complex. Teaching is recognised as one of the roles that

xii *Preface*

academics will be undertaking, and we recognise unit design or redesign as being one of the roles that academics undertake as part of their teaching responsibilities. We acknowledge that not all academics will be required to plan the design of units of study or subjects. Some academics may inherit predesigned units and could be simply asked to deliver to the plan by their departmental or school head.

Nevertheless, we believe that some level of planning and coordination may be necessary to satisfy the fundamental responsibility that is assigned to a teacher – the responsibility to guide the process of learning, make students feel accountable for doing the work of learning, and ensure that students demonstrate evidence of attainment of intended learning outcomes.

We hope that this guide will be useful as a just-in-time resource to plan, reflect and review the quality performance of a unit for making ongoing improvements to the curriculum and teaching and learning practices, and thereby student learning and experience.

References

Biggs, J.B. & Tang, C.S.-K. 2011. *Teaching for Quality Learning at University: What the student does*, 4th edn. The Society for Research into Higher Education (SRHE) and Open University Press, Maidenhead, Berkshire.

Boud, D. & Associates 2010, *Assessment 2020: Seven propositions for assessment reform in higher education*, Australian Learning and Teaching Council, Sydney, Australia.

Krathwohl, D. 2002, A revision of Bloom's Taxonomy: An overview. *Theory into Practice*, vol. 41, no. 4, pp. 212–218.

Toohey, S. 2008, *Designing Courses for Higher Education*, The Society for Research into Higher Education (SRHE) and Open University Press, Maidenhead, Berkshire.

1 Analysing the context for effective unit design

Introduction

Educational programmes also known as degree courses in higher education come in all shapes, sizes and formats. They range from certificate courses through to higher degrees by research. For the purpose of this book, we define a course as a coursework degree programme that leads to a qualification of some sort. A clear set of units of study, with varying levels of knowledge and skills complexity, and outcomes make up a course. Successful completion of these deliberately structured units of study provides a student with a credit point value. A student must accumulate all the prescribed credit points as well as meet the course rules or criteria in order complete their course. Units of study within these coursework degree courses can be designed for individual learners, or for a small or a large group of learners. A unit of study can be quite complex and multifaceted depending on its purpose and the context in which it is to be delivered.

With over 1.5 million students enrolled in higher education degree courses across Australia (Australian Government Department of Education and Training 2020), a challenge for university education these days is to educate the individual in the era of mass higher education. Universities are expected to deliver personalised learning and teaching experience, improve student participation, retention and success rates, and create an inclusive and supportive learning environment. Often, universities capture their vision for student learning in aspirational learning journeys that cater for the individual student's needs. They aim to satisfy the various learning approaches that students may take during their course of study, and how learning can be wrapped around their family, social and work commitments.

However, the question of the *value* of university education is loaded on the academic team that is involved in the design and management of a degree course, and the challenge of tackling that question is passed to the academic or teaching team that is charged with leading the design or redesign of a unit of study. Unit designers including teaching academics, teaching and learning and curriculum design experts in central teaching and learning support areas, and professional content developers constantly grapple with paying mind to the

2 *Analysing the context*

"what are" and "what could be" approaches that deliver a personalised, engaging and a rewarding course learning experience.

These challenges call upon the increasing importance in the way academics intentionally design degree courses and units of study, define learning outcomes, develop and deliver learning and assessment activities, and plan education support that meets the overall aims and outcomes of the course. This approach to learning and learning experience design is often referred to as a "whole of course approach" or "coherent course design" (Lawson 2015). Coherent course design involves identifying the purpose of the unit in the broader context of the course, and then making choices about what, when, and how to teach within units.

Unit design involves *deliberate and careful* planning and development of curriculum, learning, teaching and assessment for delivery. It takes into consideration the characteristics of learners, the environment in which they learn, and the outcomes we want them to achieve as a result of successfully completing the unit. According to Toohey (2008, p. 44), designing a unit requires careful consideration of a fundamental question: "*What is most important for these students to know and how might they best learn it?*" Unit designers are frequently called upon to make decisions about how to engage students in the learning and assessment process, and how to provide them with meaningful and actionable feedback for learning and achieving the Intended Learning Outcomes (ILOs) defined at both unit and course level.

Historical perspectives on course and unit design

Not that long ago, courses were put together as a collection of individual units. Individual academic caretakers, often referred to as unit chairs, coordinators or chief examiners, were responsible for developing the details of content, teaching and assessment as they saw fit. Often, a new unit caretaker or a teaching team member was given the unit documented in the form of a syllabus that needed to be covered. The problem with this approach was that it did not provide an incoming academic staff member with adequate information about the broader context of the course, or internal and external factors that influenced curriculum design in the first place.

Dewey's "Reflex Arc" paper (2008) first published in 1896, applied functionalism to education, in which he wrote that the question of education is the question of taking hold of (a pupil's) activities, for giving them direction. He argued that learning needs to be framed as a cumulative, progressive process in which inquirers move from the dissatisfying phase of doubt toward another marked by the satisfying resolution of a problem amidst other ongoing activities in a larger environment.

The works of Entwistle and Entwistle (1970), Perry (1970), Pask (1976), Marton and Säljö (1976) and Biggs (1987), which are concerned with improving student learning, have remained the cornerstone of much of the investigation into student development that followed. These works have influenced rethinking that resulted in many radical higher education curricular changes at both course and unit level. Research into the nature of student learning and the observation that good

Analysing the context 3

teaching promotes *active* learning has inspired many teaching strategies including problem-based, project-based, case-based and scenario-based learning.

Biggs and Tang (2011) emphasise that good teaching is about focusing on what the student does and not about focusing on what the student *is* or what the *teacher* does. The teacher, according to Biggs and Tang, merely organises the teaching and learning context, so that all students are more likely to use higher-order learning processes to complete the required learning. Organising the learning context requires constant and consistent reflection by the teacher about whether the student activities lead to appropriate learning and how the student could be supported in their learning process. The teacher is concerned with how learning can be measured and what feedback is timely and appropriate for improving learning. While Biggs and Tang have focused on *constructive alignment* of learning outcomes, assessment and teaching strategies to inspire good teaching, curriculum design often contains the blueprint for effective alignment, which promotes deep and meaningful student learning.

Factors influencing unit design

If you have worked in the Australian Higher Education sector or if you have been a keen observer, you may know that the Australian higher education system, which is made up of universities, technical and further education, and other private institutions, is at the tail end of a paradigm shift from teacher-centred to learner-centred education and training. This shift is not only observable in the way higher education providers define qualifications, but also in the way the quality and performance of teaching and learning is measured. While universities play a critical role in the development of students as professionals by giving them the skills they need for future success, they are in direct competition with other universities and many subsidiary educational and business models that drive flexible and open access to learning through Massively Open Online Courses (MOOCs) for a fraction of the cost when compared with the costs of university education.

Toohey (2008) described many of the pressures for curriculum change and highlighted that integrating theory and practice has been a long-standing problem in course design in higher education. While emphasising the political and economic factors that have influenced a demand-driven skilled labour, she brought to the fore the significant pressure it exerted on university education system that could only survive by changing and providing an education that caters to the skills and jobs of the future. Consequently, curriculum in almost every university degree course has been redesigned to integrate practical and personal skill development to enable graduates to be immediately effective in the workplace. Some of the common philosophies that Toohey highlights are summarised in Table 1.1.

Another variation is Fink's (2003) model for analysing the context when designing units. He recommends five key factors to analyse the situation carefully

4   *Analysing the context*

Table 1.1 Philosophical approaches to curriculum design

No.	Approach	Characteristics
1	Traditional or discipline based	• Knowledge exists independently • Transmission from teacher to student • Goals as lists of key concepts within the discipline • Assessment is for confirmation of level of achievement and ranking • Learning resources are usually lectures and tutorials
2	Performance or systems based	• Knowledge exists if it is shown • Students follow a planned learning path leading to end point • Content is determined by professional requirements • Assessment provides feedback (diagnostic, formative, summative) • Use of many resources, instructional videos, demonstrations, laboratories
3	Cognitive	• Development of the mind and thinking skills; knowledge is personally constructed • Limited content; in depth; questioning; critical thinking • Thinking development is both goal and content • Assessment involves demonstrations of complex understanding; problem solving • Learning activities include group work, interaction and discussion
4	Personal relevance/ experiential	• Learning personally significant knowledge within the context of the discipline • Teacher is an assistant (facilitator) to student to design and carryout learning plans • Learning outcomes able to be applied to a variety of contexts • Assessment allows learners to evaluate own learning (e.g., portfolio work) • Teacher time, individual time, independent work
5	Socially critical	• Knowledge is constructed by and within historical and cultural frameworks • Learning is envisaged from a socially critical perspective to foster conceptual change • Learning outcomes in terms of level of ability to critique, to defend etc. • Assessment allows negotiation and collaboration between students and teachers • Resource intensive small-group work, community-based projects and investigations

before beginning the actual curriculum design or redesign. Analysis would involve reviewing information already known about the teaching and learning situation, as well as gathering and reviewing additional information that may not be available to make important design decisions. These factors are adapted and summarised in Table 1.2.

Table 1.2 Situational analysis for designing units

No.	Situational factor	Questions for consideration	Importance
1	Specific context of the teaching and learning situation	<ul><li>How many students are in the class?</li><li>What is the year level of the unit?</li><li>How will the unit be delivered?</li><li>What does the learning environment look like?</li><li>What infrastructure, resources and space are needed?</li><li>What study contact is expected, how long and frequent are the classes, practical sessions and online interaction?</li></ul>	Important
2	General context of the learning situation	<ul><li>What learning expectations are placed on this unit by the discipline, course or professional accreditation bodies?</li></ul>	Important
3	Nature of the content	<ul><li>Is the content theoretical, practical or a combination?</li><li>Is the content convergent or divergent?</li><li>Are there important changes or controversies occurring within the field?</li></ul>	Useful
4	Characteristics of the learner	<ul><li>What is the life situation of the learners (e.g., working, family, professional goals)?</li><li>What prior knowledge, skills, experiences and initial feelings do students have about this unit?</li><li>What are their learning goals, expectations and preferred learning styles</li></ul>	Useful
5	Characteristics of the teacher	<ul><li>What beliefs and values does the teacher have about teaching and learning?</li><li>What is the teacher's attitude towards the subject area and students?</li><li>What level of knowledge or familiarity does the teacher have with in the field of study?</li><li>What are the teacher's strengths and vulnerabilities in teaching?</li></ul>	Useful

Challenges for effective unit design

A main challenge for academics who are involved in unit design can be determining and aligning their own personal beliefs and philosophy of teaching, learning and assessment with that of others teaching in the degree course and establishing a common course philosophy and design principles. One approach is to consider and begin curriculum design by analysing issues and perspectives on learning. Ramsden (2003) captures five fundamental issues that need to be addressed when designing units for higher education courses. These issues are summarised in Table 1.3.

6 *Analysing the context*

Table 1.3 Issues and perspectives on learning: applying theory to design practice

No.	Issues	Teacher's perspective	Learner's perspective
1	Goals and structure	What do I want my students to learn in this unit, and how can I express my goals to them and make these goals clear to my colleagues and myself?	Why is it important for me to learn this unit? What value will this unit add to my degree course?
2	Teaching strategies	How should I arrange teaching and learning so that students have the greatest chance of learning what I want them to learn?	How will the teacher help me develop key knowledge, skills and techniques involved in the unit? How am I expected to study?
3	Assessment	How can I find out whether students have learned that I hoped they would learn?	What am I expected to do? What are the assessment tasks that I need to complete in this unit?
4	Evaluation	How can I estimate the effectiveness of my teaching, and use the information I gather to improve it?	What feedback will I get? What support can I get to be successful in learning what my teacher wants me to learn in this unit?
5	Accountability and education development	How should the answers to 1–4 guide measurement and improvements to the quality of higher education?	How will my feedback be used to alleviate any uncertainty and confusion around expectations? How should I demonstrate the learning outcomes that I have attained?

Teaching academics who are charged with leading unit design work are usually required to work within the framework of a course, and an agreed set of goals for which academic and administrative considerations can be key drivers. Academic considerations can include the need for a new unit within a course in order to address knowledge or skills gap (for example, to develop foundational knowledge and skills, or an extension to provide breadth or depth of learning in a discipline area) or to influence behavioural transformations (for example, to develop skills for practice, including problem solving, critical thinking, research and professional skills) for application beyond their degree course.

Administrative considerations can include the need to address course performance and viability issues, or to address demand, student experience, student performance and progression issues, or to address professional and government accreditation requirements, or to replace similar units in several courses to minimise cost associated with unit delivery, taking into consideration available resources including staff time, equipment, and the learning environment. The current climate of clawbacks on education funding can affect a university's decision to invest resources for the design or redesign of curriculum, teaching and learning, and assessment practices, which is another important challenge for unit designers.

While the Australian Government's investment for curriculum reform has varied, their approach to formalise the measurement of graduate outcomes has only increased over the years. Teaching quality and performance is measured through evidence of student retention, course learning outcomes attained, graduate destination and employment outcomes, further study and graduate satisfaction. These measures in turn are used to represent the performance outcomes of a course and its graduates collectively. The widespread adaptation of Australian Qualifications Framework (AQF), and the legislation of Higher Education Standards Framework (Birmingham 2015) (Threshold Standards) within the Tertiary Education Quality and Standards Agency (TEQSA) Act 2011 (The Office of Parliamentary Counsel 2016) showcase the systemic higher education reform towards outcomes-based learning, which commenced in late 1970s.

Oliver (2015) and Lawson (2015) provide strategies for assuring student achievement of graduate capabilities at the expected level of standard, and emphasise that curriculum design should allow students to demonstrate evidence of learning outcomes attained. While university governance bodies have gained considerable experience in aligning unit ILOs with graduate capabilities, curriculum alignment is often seen as a compliance exercise by academics rather than something that is fundamentally beneficial for teachers and learners. In many instances, course design discussions revolve around how units can be repurposed or retrofitted to an existing or new course. Many of us seem to be unaware of, or often forget, the idea that much of the inspiration and innovation for teaching lies in the design of curriculum.

Our focus throughout this book is to change the perception that unit design is a compliance exercise. We are strongly of the belief that unit and course design are positive and creative endeavours for teachers and assessors regardless of background. The aim of our book is to provide practical advice for educational decision-making and equip those without an educational or teaching background with the knowledge of curricular, pedagogical and assessment know-how that is not focused on compliance, nor is dumbed down or beyond grasp. At the same time, we plan for the resources provided in this book to help those who have some experience in unit design to unpack the drivers for unit design and aid their reflection on the development intentional learning and teaching opportunities.

Practical perspectives and strategies for unit design: Developing a strategic rationale

Evidently, many reasons, considerations and philosophies influence design decisions and processes at a generic level. We begin with the notion that unit design helps us bring together what we teach and how we teach it in alignment with the purpose of the unit. Our experience has taught us that the unit design

8 *Analysing the context*

or redesign process should begin with academic curriculum designers defining the strategic rationale of a unit of study. Developing a strategic rationale simply means that the unit rationale is intentionally described at a strategic level. Unit design is about setting about with a purpose that serves specific needs.

There are many similarities between designing a unit and building anything with an intention. We can build a house, or rebuild a car, or anything else, without a plan, but it is far more efficient to do so with a plan and a vision of how it is to be used. Let us consider the house-building analogy. If we are involved with the full design of the house rather than just drafting a floor plan, then that house will more likely be suitably orientated on a block of land to take in the environment, the rooms will be more logically arranged, and the house will more likely be organised into effective and comfortable zones for living, dining, recreation, sleeping, etc. The process of unit design is similar; it allows the designer to test a number of ideas against the intent and requirements of various stakeholders and increase the probability of usefulness to the ultimate learner. Moreover, with good planning, there will be fewer mistakes and less wastage, and the outcome will align better with what we visualised in the first instance.

Developing the strategic rationale for a unit helps with the processes of explicitly connecting curriculum, teaching and assessment for effective student learning. We also know that our students come to us with prior knowledge, skills and interests. The strategic rationale enables us to think about how we can build on these to engage and develop our learners. The rationale also stipulates the designed intent or purpose of the unit for others to review, implement every time the unit of study is offered, and modify when necessary in the context of a degree course. We expressly explain how to evaluate the design of a unit in Chapter 7.

The development of a strategic rationale triggers an intentional process of connecting units within the course context. This is often referred to as *curriculum mapping* (Lawson 2015). However, if we go a little further to think about how the connections between teaching, learning and assessment are conceived within a unit, we can achieve internal consistency from the point of view of learner development. This is referred to as *constructive alignment*, an important aim of the unit design process. *Constructive alignment* (Biggs & Tang 2011) helps us to connect:

- The identified aims and expected learning outcomes;
- The learning activities and appropriate scaffolding which will be implemented to help students achieve these aims; and
- The way(s) in which the achievement of these outcomes will be assessed and validated.

The process of achieving internal consistency in every unit across a course is called curriculum alignment. We have identified a dozen key ideas required as questions to ask yourself when developing the strategic rationale from a student learning perspective in Table 1.4. When answering these questions, you will also be able to define the scope and priorities for the work of unit design including

Analysing the context 9

Table 1.4 Developing the strategic rationale for a unit

No.	Question	Unit designer's response
1	What is the intent of the unit, and what purpose does this unit serve within the course(s)?	
2	Who is the unit for, what outcomes must students achieve in this unit, why and at what level?	
3	What will students be able to do after successfully completing the unit?	
4	What characteristics do we want to see in our graduates? What knowledge, skills, attitudes and values will they be expected to develop?	
5	What should students know or be able to do before they study the unit?	
6	How are we able to ensure they are at this level?	
7	What content, learning activities and assessment tasks will scaffold student learning and achievement of those outcomes?	
8	What standard of performance should be required? What are the characteristics of successful performance?	
9	What methods of assessment will reliably measure student attainment of those outcomes?	
10	What method of teaching will best match the focus, that the teacher is capable of using, and that takes into account the backgrounds, experiences and knowledge levels of the learners in the learning context?	
11	What learning experiences are most appropriate to help students achieve and measure their own performance against the expected outcomes?	
12	How will we know that the unit design satisfies the intent and develops the capacity of the student to demonstrate the characteristics that we want to see in them?	

curriculum alignment and mapping. The strategic rationale thus developed will enable a teaching team to clearly articulate what the unit is about and what it can and will offer students within a course, as well as motivate students to think about what they can do with their learning beyond graduation.

Each of these questions could be answered differently according to the curriculum framework utilised by a course, discipline, department or school and the philosophical position that is embodied within that framework. For example, in a problem-based approach to learning, curriculum design may be

10 *Analysing the context*

driven by a series of challenging, open-ended problems with no one right or wrong answer. Assessment may require students to demonstrate capacity for identifying, defining and proposing solutions for real-world problems by applying problem-solving skills gained in a different situation. However, in an inquiry-based approach to learning, curriculum design may be driven by questions that prompt thinking, followed by the location, interpretation and analysis of information. Assessment may require reflection on the process to allow students to construct their own knowledge and meaning.

Further thought and planning is needed to then consider a teaching perspective in the design of units in order to provide structured and supportive learning environments irrespective of the mode of delivery – on campus, online or blended.

- How does learning occur and how is it best facilitated? What should be the role of teachers and what should be expected of students?
- What goals and outcomes are meaningful within a unit of study and how are they best expressed?
- What content is essential and what is desirable? How should it be organised for on campus, online or blended learning?
- What purpose do we need assessment to serve and what form should it take?
- What kinds of resources and infrastructure are needed to teach and assess student learning?

Philosophies and beliefs about knowledge and the nature of learning, how a body of knowledge should be taught and the best ways to teach it, can and will influence academic thinking and educational decision-making. But, the context of the course should be considered when making decisions about the education philosophy and its appropriateness for the unit, irrespective of personal philosophy or preferred pedagogical approach. It is also important to note that within courses that utilise problem-based, project-based, or inquiry-based approaches for learning, not all units may employ that approach to learning. Some units may be deliberately designed to provide a variety in learning approaches for students, to allow them to develop different learning skills, or to provide alternative environments for learning to occur.

Summary

The first step in designing a unit is to develop a strategic rationale for the unit. This step will help you analyse the course context for initiating unit design or redesign. The purpose of analysing the context for unit design is to establish the need for the unit, and to plan how to effectively design the unit of study for implementation within a degree course. The process of unit design following that is essentially about unpacking what you want your students to be able to do as a result of successfully completing the unit. For this we need to tap into their prior knowledge and skills, and design learning activities that will

Analysing the context 11

challenge students to achieve and demonstrate the learning outcomes. We have included a simple worksheet in Appendix A to document your initial analysis. This worksheet is based on following five key design principles, which we have derived from our research into unit design and tested through our own teaching and learning practice.

1   The learning intended for students within a unit should be aligned with the learning intended in the degree course and graduate outcomes. This principle ensures that students can see the big picture and make holistic connections in their field of study.
2   The design of assessment tasks should identify key criteria and standards for student performance. This principle enables both the teacher and the student to evidence the achievement of intended learning outcomes.
3   The design of learning activities should provide students opportunities for active engagement. This principle enables the teacher to scaffold student learning and enable achievement of learning outcomes, taking into consideration differences in student learning needs.
4   The design of feedback should be integrated, purposeful and actionable by the student. This principle enables planning student learning and supporting their education and development.
5   The plan for unit evaluation should encourage the capture of pre- and post-improvement snapshot. This will enable staff to understand the effects of teaching on students' learning and make judgements about the kinds of actions necessary for improving teaching practice.

An outcome of the unit design process is to determine the full range of learning intended for students to achieve. While the desired outcomes that we have of our students have broadened considerably, we need to determine how our curriculum will look in action when compared with the espoused curriculum. That is, we need to translate our design intentions into teaching and learning actions. Not only should assessment practice be learner-centred and based on outcomes, but teaching should also be directed at achieving the desired learning outcomes in terms of student learning. Learning occurs when the student reflects on their outcomes. Timely feedback on their engagement in the learning process and the outcomes that they have achieved enhances their opportunity to plan further learning and development.

The measure of learning success from a student's perspective can be a pass, credit, distinction or high distinction. However, from an academic perspective the measure of success is what a student can do even if they just pass the unit. Thinking about what students must be able to do even if they only pass the unit is not about reducing the intellectual or academic rigour to make the unit manageable for those students who wish to expend the least amount of effort required to pass. Rather, it is about determining and articulating the minimum academic standards clearly and consistently to the students. The next chapter deals with how to develop and communicate ILOs. If a set of ILOs already

12   *Analysing the context*

exists, then the redesign process could start with an evaluation of the ILOs and the associated learning and teaching plans.

References

Australian Government Department of Education and Training 2020, 'Higher Education Statistics', at http://highereducationstatistics.education.gov.au.

Biggs, J.B. 1987, *Student Approach to Learning and Studying*. Research Monograph, Australian Council for Educational Research, Melbourne, Australia.

Biggs, J.B., & Tang, C.S.-K. 2011. *Teaching for Quality Learning at University: What the student does*, 4th edn, The Society for Research into Higher Education (SRHE) and Open University Press, Maidenhead, Berkshire.

Birmingham, S. 2015, *Higher Education Standards Framework (Threshold Standards) 2015*, Department of Education and Training, Australian Government, Federal Register of Legislative Instruments.

Dewey, J. 2008 (1896), *The Early Works of John Dewey, 1882–1898*, Electronic edn, vol. 5, 38 vols., The Collected Works of John Dewey, 1882–1953 (2nd release). Southern Illinois University Press, Carbondale and Edwardsville.

Entwistle, N. & Entwistle, D. 1970, 'The relationships between personality, study methods and academic performance', *British Journal of Educational Psychology*, vol. 40, no. 2, pp. 132–143.

Fink, D. 2003, *Creating Significant Learning Experiences: An integrated approach to designing college courses*, Jossey-Bass, San Francisco, CA.

Lawson, R. 2015, *Curriculum Design for Assuring Learning – Leading the Way: Final report*, Office for Learning and Teaching, Department of Education, Sydney, Australia.

Marton, F. & Säljö, R. 1976, 'On qualitative differences in learning: Outcome and process', *British Journal of Educational Psychology*, vol. 46, no. 1, pp. 4–11.

Oliver, B. 2015, *Assuring Graduate Capabilities: Evidencing levels of achievement for graduate employability*, Deakin University, Sydney, Australia.

Pask, G. 1976, 'Styles and strategies of learning', *British Journal of Educational Psychology*, vol. 46, no. 2, pp. 128–148.

Perry, W. 1970, *Forms of Intellectual and Ethical Development in the College Years: A scheme*, Holt Rinehart and Winston, New York.

Ramsden, P. 2003, *Learning to Teach in Higher Education*, 2nd edn, Routledge Falmer, New York.

The Office of Parliamentary Counsel 2016, *Tertiary Education Quality and Standards Agency Act 2011*, Department of Education and Training, Australian Government.

Toohey, S. 2008, *Designing Courses for Higher Education*, The Society for Research into Higher Education (SRHE) and Open University Press, Maidenhead, Berkshire.

2 Designing unit learning outcomes

Introduction

For some years now, universities and academics have been under significant pressure from industries and governments to provide educational experiences that enable graduates to have an outward focus and the ability to apply the knowledge and skills that they have developed to a wide range of jobs in their future careers. Regularly shown by census data, and argued by social scientists and economists, it is highly likely that individuals with better skills and qualifications generally enjoy lower unemployment rates, higher wages and better quality of life (Chetty et al. 2011; Department of Education and Training 2018).

It is no surprise that the global focus has turned to articulating learning outcomes for higher education students to provide them with the skills they need to succeed in the workplace. The emphasis on work-readiness of graduates is supported by a shift in focus from content-based learning to an outcome-based education, which is often referred to as a "paradigm shift" in higher education. Paradigms, as described by Guba and Lincoln (1994), are basic belief systems that guide action. Originally coined by Spady (1994), Outcome-Based Education (OBE) facilitates our thinking and ability to decrease the disconnect between teaching and learning, graduate skills and employer expectations. It is now well accepted in many developed and developing nations that outcome-based education enables us to help students to set and achieve goals that are beyond just unit and course completion.

While writing learning outcomes may have come under fire at times as representative of some progressivist educational fad, it actually poses very little threat and a great deal of benefit for more conservative educators. So, *what are learning outcomes? How can we define them better to our students? How can we use them for developing resources for learning and teaching?* These questions are at the heart of this chapter. Our aim is to help unit designers, teachers and assessors articulate what their students can and will be able to do, upon completion of a unit of study, that they otherwise would not have been able to demonstrate.

14   *Designing unit learning outcomes*

The purpose of learning outcomes

The notion of learning outcomes is not new. For more than 20 years, Australian Universities in particular have been referring to Intended Learning Outcomes (or simply ILOs) when setting overall objectives for their education and training. In simple terms, ILOs are *statements that outline the knowledge and skills that students can demonstrate as a result of successful completion of study.* ILOs are more than merely goals for learning – they are expectations that drive learner behaviour and action for development and achievement (Biggs & Tang 2011).

Many governments and professional accreditation bodies subscribe to UNESCO's *four pillars of learning,* which enable the alignment of various international qualifications frameworks and educational systems ranging from primary through to higher education (Delors 1996). These pillars are:

- **Learning to know** (by combining a sufficiently broad general knowledge with the opportunity to work in depth on a small number of subjects and learning to learn, so as to benefit from the opportunities education provides throughout life);
- **Learning to do** (by developing not only occupational skills, but also more broadly, the competence to deal with many situations and work in teams);
- **Learning to live together** (by developing an understanding of other people and an appreciation of interdependence – carrying out joint projects, learning to manage conflicts, in a spirit of respect for the values of pluralism, mutual understand and peace);
- **Learning to be** (so as to better develop one's personality and ability to act with even greater autonomy, judgement and personal responsibility).

The four UNESCO pillars of learning were first developed by Jaques Delors for the International Commission on Education for the 21st Century report (1996). In this report, Delors highlighted that:

> formal education systems tend to emphasise the acquisition of knowledge to the detriment of other types of learning: but it is vital now to conceive education in a more encompassing fashion. Such a vision should inform and guide educational reforms and policy, in relation to both contents and to methods.
>
> (Delors 1996, p. 37)

While highlighting the role higher education plays in the prosperity of a nation, Delors implied that its strength and ability to meet the demands of the future lies in the vision it has for lifelong education and integration in a society where degree courses offer varied learning opportunities to meet learners where they are, and where they want to go.

Designing unit learning outcomes 15

The UNESCO pillars of learning have significant influence on how we design courses and units within, and how we measure learner success. Qualification frameworks such as the Australian Qualifications Framework (AQF) or the European Qualifications Framework (EQF) categorise these pillars of learning as knowledge, skills, competencies and attitudes to formulate educational outcomes in order to measure learner success and curriculum quality at various levels of education and training.

The AQF recognises the need for increasingly complex learning and cognitive function and provides a pathway for student progression across a range of qualification levels (commonly called AQF levels) through specific learning outcomes for each level and qualification type. Learning outcomes are useful, as they provide the basis for individuals to progress through education and training and gain recognition for their prior learning and experience. A challenge is to use action verbs in ILO statements as critical indicators of the student engagement and required performance at a specific level. This will be the focus of our chapter.

In the context of Australian universities, learner success is measured in terms of the ability of the student to evidence the ILOs that they have achieved within each unit and at the course level for successful course completion. The testamur that students receive on successful completion of their course validates the type of qualification, signals the level of attainment of that qualification, and supports their mobility for further education and training or their career pursuits.

The quality of a degree course is measured in terms of

> the design and content of each course of study, expected learning outcomes, the methods for assessment of those outcomes, the extent of students' achievement of learning outcomes, and also takes account of emerging developments in the field of education, modes of delivery, the changing needs of students and identified risks to the quality of the course of study.
>
> (Birmingham 2015)

This statement clearly acknowledges the central role that expected or intended learning outcomes play in delivering a course of quality. In short, they answer the question: "How will the teaching team ensure that all graduates have achieved the minimum standard against the ILOs at the course level?"

Thus, the three main purposes of ILOs are to evidence learner performance against unit and course expectations, provide a pathway for student progression and gain recognition for their prior learning and experience. As such, ILOs propose the value of university education to student and highlights what the return will be for their investment of time, effort and money in gaining something that they do not already have or cannot acquire without the support of an expert teacher or facilitator.

16 *Designing unit learning outcomes*

The knack of writing learning outcomes

In our roles as academic developers, we have fielded frequent criticism about the need to rewrite course objectives, or content lists, as ILOs. We argue, as do others, that there are valuable benefits of articulating ILOs as opposed to teaching objectives or lists of topics, something which is still common in unit handbooks/outlines.

ILOs explicitly acknowledge the *student's* role in learning, whereas statements of knowledge to be learned do not. The latter tend to imply that knowledge will simply be put into a student's head, with no clarity about how the knowledge is to be used. Pedagogical implications are not considered, and thus the objectives provide little in the way of guidance for teaching academics.

There is a significant conceptual difference between unit objectives *and* learning outcomes; this is not a simple matter of petty semantics. ILOs enable teachers to inform students about what will be assessed, the minimum standard expected in each assessment task, the method of assessment and the learning activities that will support students in their development of knowledge and skills required to complete the assessment task.

The knack of writing effective ILOs is to focus on the *output* factors, that is, what a student will be able to do as a result of studying, indicating that they have been assessed as having successfully completed the unit. Toohey (2008) lists characteristics of effective learning outcomes. According to her, they:

- are meaningful, not trivial;
- place the development of the learner and the learner's skills within the context of the subject/discipline;
- consider what students should be able to do (or demonstrate they can do);
- allow for the development of new skills or betterment of existing skills; and
- are memorable and kept low in number.

We can use this list to evaluate and revise existing ILOs. Consider the following example, which is real-life makeover of unit objectives to ILOs based on these characteristics of effectiveness.

Example 1:

Original

The objective of this unit is to:

1   introduce the wider context of professional engineering: at one level dealing with the interplay between the professions, industry and the community, and at another level, with the interplay between analysis, synthesis, and management processes;

Designing unit learning outcomes 17

2 provide a rationale and foundation for future subjects in engineering and engineering management through group projects involving problem-based learning.

Revised

On successful completion of this unit, students will be able to:

1 explain and correctly apply the general engineering method of problem solving;
2 explain and apply the concept of "the triple bottom line" (economic, social and environmental factors) to evaluate potential engineering solutions;
3 apply the engineering code of ethics in the context of engineering practice;
4 apply basic project management concepts and tools to a design project, including working effectively as part of a team;
5 communicate effectively in both written and oral form, including using the appropriate academic conventions of the discipline.

In the revised version (using outcomes rather than objectives), the focus is on student learning, and more importantly, what students should be able to do during, and as a consequence of, their learning. These ILOs can guide those teaching into the unit, as they are more specific. Each of the outcomes is distinctly essential to the unit and implies development of students' knowledge and skills. ILOs written in such a way inform assessment design, as well as the design of learning activities such that students can demonstrate their learning progress. Unit designers' articulation of the unit outcomes will guide teaching and students' learning not only within the unit, but also within the course and beyond.

Our advice is to stay away from using "understand" as a verb describing student learning outcomes. The term is too ambiguous: if your students understand something, how will they show you that understanding? It is far more efficient to define how they will convince you that they understand, and your assessment and teaching and learning activities will be defined. We have also come across "demonstrate understanding". Again, for the same reason, this is not a good choice of words because it is too ambiguous. It will be better to state what students must do in order to demonstrate that understanding. It will be a more accurate statement, and therefore measurable. We are all probably familiar with "appreciate" used in such statements. The trouble is that appreciation is even less measurable than understanding and can therefore be easily fudged. We all have different motivations and dispositions. There is a fundamental difference between what you hope students must do, and what they will do. Stick to things you can control. Here is another example of a revised set of ILOs:

18 *Designing unit learning outcomes*

Example 2:

Original

A student successfully completing this unit will have:

1   an understanding of the nature of the real number system, through well-founded skills;
2   skills in algebra and an understanding of how these are based on properties of number systems;
3   an appreciation of the applicability of mathematical theory and skills;
4   knowledge of the role coordinate geometry plays in linking algebra and geometry.

Revised

On successful completion of this unit, the students will be able to:

1   explain the key defining features of the real number system;
2   apply algebraic methods using the properties of number systems;
3   apply a variety of mathematical theories and skills to the solution of real-world problems;
4   create meaningful links between algebra and geometry by applying key principles of coordinate geometry.

The second set of ILOs is focused on what the student can do, not what they might know. Verbs are used to indicate what these things are, informing assessment and rubric design, as well as learning experience design. All of the ILOs can be objectively measurable. Moreover, care has been taken to "pitch" the ILOs at the levels of understanding required for students to successfully complete the unit. These, of course, will be dependent upon the nature of the unit, and its place in the course structure (early/first year, intermediate or later/capstone, for example). More examples can be found in Biggs and Tang (2011). If sourcing ideas from the internet, apply the principles discussed here. Meanwhile, we provide some individual examples below in Table 2.1. In Examples 1 and 2 above, and again in Table 2.1, we applied Toohey's characteristics of good learning outcomes to evaluate and revise existing outcomes. We did so by deliberately featuring verbs indicating the level and type of student performance that would indicate to us their achievement of the unit and course intentions.

Writing ILOs from scratch

In the higher education sector, the work of John Biggs has had considerable impact, and it is his work with colleague Catherine Tang that informs our approach to unit and course design. His work is among the most applied of any

Table 2.1 Examples of ILOs pre- and post-revision

Original outcome	Comment	Revised outcome	Comment
... gain experience in applying the quadratic formula to the solution of problems	This is more about what the course offers and reads more like a tutorial activity than an outcome. Gaining experience does not necessarily imply learning. This is not measurable	... apply the quadratic formula in order to solve problems	This clearly states what the students will do, is measurable, and informs the task design This can be at a level appropriate to 1st- or 3rd-year students, depending on the problems and their complexity
... discuss the elements of unit design	This is more like a learning activity, not an outcome, and is too broad/vague. Any unenlightened person can "discuss" anything! This is not measurable, nor does it clearly relate to the development of new skills	... explain how the various elements of unit design contribute to students' learning	This is more in line with the intention of the unit It is meaningful, assumes development, and is measurable Any task associated with this outcome, will require students to "explain ..." If that is not what I want students to be able to do, then I can change the verb This is probably a low-level outcome. A higher-level outcome would ask students to design those elements
... understand how combustion engines work	This is too broad. "Understand" is not specifically measurable	... name the parts, and explain the function of the parts, of a combustion engine	This is more explicit and informs the task design. If students can do these things at a level you expect, then they will have achieved this objective of the course This is probably a low-level outcome (early in a degree). A higher-level outcome would probably ask students to design a combustion engine based on this understanding

20 *Designing unit learning outcomes*

in the field of teaching and learning in higher education. Importantly, his *constructive alignment* (introduced in Chapter 1) underpins the development of ILOs:

> 'Constructive' comes from the constructivist theory that learners use their own activity to construct their knowledge as interpreted through their own existing schemata. 'Alignment' is a principle in curriculum theory that assessment tasks should be aligned to what it is intended to be learned, as in criterion-referenced assessment. Constructive alignment extends in a practical way Shuell's statement that 'what the student does is actually more important in determining what is learned than what the teacher does' (1986: 429). The intended outcomes specify the activity that students should engage if they are to achieve the intended outcome as well as the content the activity refers to. The teacher's tasks are to set up a learning environment that encourages the student to perform those learning activities, and to assess student performances against the intended learning outcomes.
>
> (Biggs & Tang 2011, p. 97)

The skills and capabilities that a student must develop as a result of studying a unit should be aligned with course-level or graduate-level learning outcomes, meaning that students can demonstrate a variety of skills they have gained over the course of their degree to potential employers and industry groups. Biggs and Tang (2011) provide a useful analysis of the differences in learning outcomes at various levels – graduate, course and unit. As we highlighted in Chapter 1, we need to able to articulate learning outcomes at all levels, and they need to be aligned such that unit-level ILOs feed up to course-level ILOs, which in turn feed up to graduate ILOs to achieve *internal consistency or coherence in course design.*

Constructive alignment is achieved using a mapping process, a practice that has become very familiar to many teaching academics, academic curriculum designers and academic administrators. Following principles of outcome-based education, the process is termed *backwards mapping* in that we start with the graduate outcomes, formulate course outcomes, and then formulate individual unit outcomes. So too, within unit design, we start with unit ILOs, then develop assessments, and then develop teaching and learning activities rather than designing in the other direction. At the unit level, this essentially involves a shifting of focus from what the unit might do for the student to what a student might do as a result of their engagement with the unit.

An essential statement to complete is "As a result of successfully completing this unit, students will be able to: ...", although there are several minor variations to this statement. In the examples above, we have used "On successful completion of this unit, students will be able to: ...".

Take the example, "At the completion of this Unit, successful students can: Map the environment of an engineering business to perform a situational analysis of engineering activities". Note that this *leading statement* (or stem) highlights the action expected of students when they pass the unit. The *action verb* "Map" that follows this stem should indicate specifically what you want students to do. This enables them to consider how they will approach learning in the unit, and how they will use the scheduled learning activities, resources, interactions (with the resources, teachers and peers) to plan their learning actions. The *focus and/or context* of their activity is indicated next to the action verb. In this case, a student is expected to map the environment of an engineering business to perform a situational analysis of engineering activities. This highlights the *process, product or outcome* of the action and *any condition* that may need to be satisfied for completing the action.

Essentially, the learning outcome statement is composed of a leading statement, the action verb, the focus or the context of the intended action, and any condition that must be applied or satisfied by the learner in order to achieve the intended outcome. By following this simple step, you can construct outcomes that create the foundation for the development of your unit. Use our ILO checker and ILO development sheet to improve your unit ILOs. These can be found in Appendices B and C.

Unpacking learning from taxonomies of verbs

Bloom's Taxonomy has been a widely accepted approach for categorising intended cognitive processes. The original taxonomy of educational objectives created by Benjamin Bloom and Associates (1956) specifies three domains: (1) the *cognitive* domain, which relates to mental skills or knowledge; (2) the *psychomotor* domain, which refers to manual, dexterous and physical skills; and (3) the *affective* domain, which relates to feelings, attitudes and emotional aspects of learning.

These domains were created to categorise and promote higher-order cognitive processes in terms of (1) knowledge (cognitive and intellectual abilities); (2) skills (psychomotor); and (3) attitudes (affective). Bloom further classified the cognitive domain into six major categories – knowledge, comprehension, application, analysis, synthesis and evaluation – of cognitive process in a sequential order of difficulty to imply that one process must be mastered before the next one can take place.

Because we are focused on unpacking what students should *do* to learn, the verbs that describe their action should be chosen deliberately. Table 2.2 provides a list of verbs that generally refer to actions associated with the intended cognitive process. The verbs here are an adaptation of Anderson and Krathwohl's (2001) *revised Bloom's Taxonomy* and Krathwohl's subsequent explanation of that revision (2002) in an attempt to remove unidimensionality of the knowledge framework from the *original taxonomy*.

Although the cognitive process and knowledge dimensions are represented as hierarchical steps, the distinctions between categories are not always clear-cut. For example, all procedural knowledge is not necessarily more abstract than all conceptual knowledge; and a learning outcome that involves a student

22 *Designing unit learning outcomes*

Table 2.2 Action verbs for the cognitive processes dimension

Remember	Retrieve relevant knowledge from long-term memory	Define, describe, draw, find, identify, label, list, match, name, quote, recall, recite, recognise, tell, write
Understand	Construct meaning from instructional messages, including oral, written and graphical communication	Classify, compare, conclude, demonstrate, discuss, exemplify, explain, identify, illustrate, infer, interpret, paraphrase, predict, report, summarise
Apply	Carry out or use a procedure in a given situation	Apply, change, choose, compute, dramatise, execute, implement, interview, prepare, produce, role play, select, show, transfer, use
Analyse	Break material into constituent parts and determine how parts relate to one another and to an overall structure or purpose	Analyse, attribute, characterise, classify, compare, contrast, debate, deconstruct, deduce, differentiate, discriminate, distinguish, examine, organise, outline, relate, research, separate, structure
Evaluate	Make judgement based on criteria and standards	Appraise, argue, assess, check, choose, conclude, critique, decide, evaluate, judge, justify, monitor, predict, prioritise, prove, rank, rate, select
Create	Put elements together to form a coherent whole; reorganise into a new pattern or structure	Compose, construct, create, design, develop, generate, hypothesise, invent, make, perform, plan, produce

Adapted from Anderson and Krathwohl (2001, pp. 67–68) and Krathwohl (2002, p. 215).

analysing or evaluating may require thinking skills that are no less complex than one that involves creating. Nevertheless, it is generally understood that lower-order thinking skills are subsumed by and provide the foundation for higher-order thinking skills.

Krathwohl (2002) rationalised Bloom's Taxonomy into a two-dimensional framework: *knowledge and cognitive processes* to refer to students' cognitive processes associated developing and working with knowledge. Naming it a taxonomy for teaching, learning and assessment, he drew attention away from the static notion of educational objectives and pointed to a dynamic concept of the classification to explain how the knowledge dimension intersected with the cognitive process dimension to specify ILOs for different levels of cognition- factual, conceptual, procedural and metacognitive.

Table 2.3, which is adapted from Krathwohl's work, can be used to develop a visual representation of outcomes, activities and assessment within a unit or a

Table 2.3 Krathwohl's two-dimensional cognitive processes framework

	Remember	Understand	Apply	Analyse	Evaluate	Create
	Retrieve relevant knowledge from long-term memory	Construct meaning from instructional messages, including oral, written and graphical communication	Carry out or use a procedure in a given situation	Break material into constituent parts and determine how parts relate to one another and to overall structure or purpose	Make judgement based on criteria and standards	Put elements together to form a coherent whole; reorganise into a new pattern or structure
Factual knowledge • Terminology • Specific details and elements						
Conceptual knowledge • Classifications and categories • Principles and generalisations • Theories, models and structures						
Procedural knowledge • Subject specific skills and algorithms, techniques and methods • Determining when to use appropriate procedures						
Metacognitive • Strategic knowledge • Knowledge about cognitive tasks (including appropriate contextual and conditional knowledge) • Self-knowledge						

24 *Designing unit learning outcomes*

course, which can then be examined for learning emphasis, curriculum alignment or missed educational opportunities.

John Biggs's SOLO (Structure of Observed Learning Outcome) Taxonomy (Biggs & Collis 1982) is also very popular. It is based on the structural complexity of the student's response to an assessment task. In other words, it is focused on the qualities of the work submitted for assessment. Five levels of "mastery" are distinguished in this seminal work (Biggs & Tang 2011, pp. 351–352), and verbs associated with each level (except prestructural) (Biggs & Tang 2011, p. 123) are provided in Table 2.4.

Taxonomies such as Bloom's or SOLO can be used to locate a verb which describes the cognitive process (knowledge and intellectual ability) the unit designer intends to assess. While both taxonomies are extremely useful, these verbs do not address expectations of learning beyond knowledge development

Table 2.4 SOLO Taxonomy verbs

Prestructural	The task is not attacked appropriately; the student hasn't understood the point	
Unistructural	One or a few aspects of the task are picked up and used (understanding as nominal)	Count, define, draw, find, identify, imitate label, match, memorise, name, order, quote, recall, recite, recognise, tell, write
Multistructural	Several aspects of the task are learned but are treated separately (understanding as knowing about)	Classify, compute, describe, discuss, illustrate, list, narrate, outline, report, select, separate sequence
Relational	The components are integrated into a coherent whole, with each part contributing to the overall meaning (understanding as appreciating relationships)	Analyse, apply, argue, characterise, compare, conclude, construct, contrast, debate, differentiate, examine, explain, integrate, make a case, organise, paraphrase, plan, predict, review, review and rewrite, solve a problem summarise (précis), transfer, translate
Extended abstract	The integrated whole at the relational level is reconceptualised at a higher level of abstraction, which enables generalisation to a new topic or area, or is turned reflexively on oneself (understanding as far transfer, and as involving metacognition)	Compose, create, generalise, generate, hypothesise, invent, make an original case, originate, prove from first principles, reflect, solve from first principles, theorise

Designing unit learning outcomes 25

Table 2.5 Action verbs categories

Developing psychomotor skills	_Strengthening problem-finding and solving capabilities_	_Changing attitudes, values, beliefs and feelings_
Adjust	Analyse	Admit
Alter	Calculate	Adopt
Apply	Categorise	Advocate
Arrange	Change	Augment
Assemble	Clarify	Bargain
Build	Compose	Challenge
Classify	Confine	Choose
Conduct	Consider	Collaborate
Construct	Create	Defend
Demonstrate	Deconstruct	Dispute
Design	Determine	Endorse
Detect	Diagnose	Express
Draft	Discover	Judge
Draw	Distinguish	Justify
Exhibit	Enhance	Lead
Extract	Evaluate	Maintain
Install	Examine	Manage
Isolate	Practice	Motivate
Locate	Predict	Persuade
Manipulate	Prioritise	Protest
Operate	Propose	Question
Perform	Search	Reflect

Adapted from Caffarella (2002, p. 171).

and intellectual skills. Table 2.5 provides a set of verbs for developing psychomotor skills, strengthening problem-finding and problem-solving skills and developing transformative learning, which can be used to write learning outcomes and assess student achievement of those outcomes. However, it is imperative that you consider what the learner is expected to know and do with the learning opportunity that you provide them with; the conditions under which the learning is to be demonstrated; and the standards for minimum acceptable performance.

Summary

Whether we are developing courses or units, we need to have clear goals in mind and justify the rationale and context that underpins its design. Otherwise, it will be challenging to execute our plans for student learning. Unit designers'

26 *Designing unit learning outcomes*

articulation of the unit outcomes will guide teaching and students' learning not only within the unit, but also within the course and beyond.

In higher education, there is an expectation that a student will pursue increasingly complex learning and therefore will be able to function at a higher cognitive level as they progress through their course. As we highlighted in Chapter 1, units are designed within a course for a number of reasons. The strategic rationale for a unit provides us with information about whether the unit is at introductory, intermediate, or advanced level within a course. Knowing the rationale or being able to define the rationale helps us to identify the level of cognitive process or standard that a student should be able to achieve up on successful unit completion for progression within the course and beyond graduation.

As Biggs and Tang (2011) point out, it is what the student *does* during the unit that allows them to achieve ILOs. The ILO statement should therefore be conceived for student application (later in their professional life), rather than merely listing the unit activities. As learning outcomes are to be clearly stated *before* teaching takes place, teaching should be designed to engage students in learning activities that maximises their chances of achieving those outcomes. Assessment tasks should be designed to enable clear judgements as to how well those outcomes have been attained. Well-written ILOs can be used as criteria for assessment within a rubric that can be used to clarify standards of achievement.

References

Anderson, L. & Krathwohl, D. 2001, *A Taxonomy for Learning, Teaching and Assessing: A revision of Bloom's Taxonomy of educational objectives*, Longman, New York.

Biggs, J.B. & Collis, K.F. 1982, *Evaluating the Quality of Learning: The SOLO Taxonomy*, Academic Press, New York.

Biggs, J.B., & Tang, C.S.-K. 2011, *Teaching for Quality Learning at University: What the student does*, 4th edn, The Society for Research into Higher Education (SRHE) and Open University Press, Maidenhead, Berkshire.

Birmingham, S. 2015, *Higher Education Standards Framework (Threshold Standards) 2015*, Department of Education and Training, Australian Government, Federal Register of Legislative Instruments.

Bloom, B.S. (ed.), Engelhart, M.D., Furst, E.J., Hill, W.H., & Krathwohl, D.R. 1956, *Taxonomy of educational objectives: The classification of educational goals. Handbook 1: Cognitive domain*, David McKay, New York.

Caffarella, R.S. 2002, *Planning Programs for Adult Learners: A practical guide for educators, trainers and staff developers*, 2nd edn, vol. 1, Jossey-Bass, New York.

Chetty, R., Friedman, J., Hilger, N., Saez, E., Schanzenbach, D.W. & Yagan, D. 2011, 'How does your kindergarten classroom affect your earnings? Evidence from Project Star', *The Quarterly Journal of Economics*, vol. 126, no. 4, pp. 1593–1660.

Delors, J. 1996, *Learning: the treasure within*, report to UNESCO of the International Commission on Education for the Twenty-first Century.

Department of Education and Training 2018, *Through Growth to Achievement: Report of the Review to Achieve Educational Excellence in Australian Schools*, Australian Government.

Guba, E. & Lincoln, Y. 1994, 'Competing paradigms in qualitative research', in *Handbook of Qualitative Research*, Sage, Thousand Oaks, CA, pp. 105–117.

Krathwohl, D. 2002, 'A revision of Bloom's Taxonomy: An overview', *Theory into Practice*, vol. 41, no. 4, pp. 212–218.

Spady, W. 1994, *Outcome-Based Education: Critical issues and answers*, American Association of School Administrators, Arlington, VA.

Toohey, S. 2008, *Designing Courses for Higher Education*, The Society for Research into Higher Education (SRHE) and Open University Press, Maidenhead, Berkshire.

3 Developing assessment methods

The nature and function of assessment

Assessing learning is an integral part of teaching. The process of assessment involves evaluation of a student's academic performance in each of the assessment tasks prescribed for a unit. The design of assessment must not be an afterthought, but a deliberate decision that allows students to demonstrate the ILOs. Assessment design, which is an important aspect of the unit design or redesign process, is done well before the design of specific learning activities. Once finalised, assessment designs are scrutinised and tested as appropriate by the relevant institutional committee prior to the unit offering to ensure fairness and consistency of assessment delivery.

A well-designed assessment task serves four main functions:

1 It motivates students and helps them to structure their academic efforts.
2 It gives students an indication of topics or skills they should concentrate for mastery.
3 It helps academics identify errors and misconceptions of students and adjust teaching to improve learning.
4 It evaluates and documents whether students have learnt what the unit intends.

At the completion of each assessment task, students are usually provided with a grade or a mark, which may count towards their final result. The view held by many that assessment drives student learning has profound implications for higher education teaching practice. However, it is important to recognise that often the mark or grade associated with an assessment task is usually what drives a student's approach to learning. Despite the nature or quality of feedback that we provide students, at times most of us have encountered students arguing for losing a mark or half a mark on an assessment piece. We would have also come across students who have the capacity to achieve higher but will only expend enough effort to achieve a pass grade. So, how could we shift this student focus and assist them evidence achievement of ILOs? How could we build their resilience and support them to develop life-long learning skills?

Characteristics of assessment

Nightingale et al. (1996) highlighted that traditional forms of assessment such as essays, reports and exams have usually focused on ranking students according to the knowledge that they gained in a unit. These methods allowed students to demonstrate knowledge in easily measurable ways so that comparisons between them were easy. Student achievements in these forms of assessment were viewed in quantitative terms – "How much do they know?" – and judgements made by assessors are often a definitive statement of the student's ability, rather than what learning outcomes were observable. These assessment methods may not support and promote what we call *authentic* learning. That is, even though students may have successfully progressed through all the assessments for their degree, they may still hold fundamental misconceptions about the principles on which the degree is based and/or be unable to practically apply those principles in the real world.

Our review of many university assessment tasks indicated that assessment designs still display these characteristics. However, research into student learning, and an increasing focus on employability skills have influenced many changes in the way assessment is practised nowadays. Assessment overall has changed in its intent, and in its methods, to allow testing and measurement of a broader range of student abilities and competencies such as communication skills, teamwork skills, critical thinking and problem-solving skills to name a few.

Regardless of the method of assessment or the form of student output, we believe that the ultimate goal of assessment design should be to ensure that each student can demonstrate evidence of ILOs attained through their engagement in learning and assessment activities. Some key features of assessment design include:

- placing assessment at the heart of the curriculum, aligned with teaching and learning activities and desired outcomes;
- developing assessment practices that focus students on learning, not just on achieving grades;
- providing feedback that is used by students to improve their work; and
- developing students' critical judgement skills and self-direction.

With these in mind we consider assessment as an essential part of any curriculum, not simply as a tool for measuring students' performance. In this chapter, we will focus only on assessment design and assessment practices that focus on student *learning*, leaving our focus on criteria and standards (and rubrics), and feedback for the next chapter.

Placing assessment at the heart of the curriculum

Assessment 2020: Seven propositions for assessment reform in higher education (Boud & Associates 2010) is a useful guide for thinking about assessment that aligns with

30 *Developing assessment methods*

high academic standards and the needs of the sector. The propositions in this guide can be applied at a range of levels, from teaching in individual units, to institution-wide approaches.

In the model of constructive alignment (Biggs & Tang 2011), learning outcomes specify the activities that students must do. Largely, learning takes place through activities in and out of class, and assessments confirm and motivate performance. This is particularly true for problem-based and practice-based learning models where assessment tasks are authentic representation of the ILOs, regardless of whether the tasks are diagnostic, formative or summative in nature. Such models and frameworks for assessment design in higher education regularly highlight that the central role of assessment is to shape learning. Any assessment activity should therefore, be conceived and designed as a learning activity – removing anything extraneous to ensure that students see value in engagement.

Three key principles for assessment design

When designing assessment tasks, we recommend three principles to be kept in mind:

- The choice of assessment method should allow for reasonable judgements to be made about the extent to which the student has achieved the ILOs of the unit and the course.
- The assessment method chosen should support real learning and achievement of the ILOs.
- The assessment workload for both students and markers should be reasonable.

These principles highlight the need for establishing a common set of curriculum practices and ensuring assessment and grading that define and protect academic standards. Many universities have defined policies and procedures to guide academics in making decisions about assessment practice. These policies and procedures often provide valuable information about the institution's philosophy and approach for assessing student learning.

Choice of assessment

Generally, student output required in assessment tasks can be divided into four categories:

- written tasks;
- oral tasks;
- performance tasks;
- design tasks.

A variety of summative assessment tasks including essays, reports, tests, presentations, portfolios, journals, theses and examinations can be useful for assessing student learning. However, the decision for the particular method of assessment to be used in a unit should be made based on their suitability for assessing ILOs. For example, if a learning outcome states that students should be able to "explain" something, multiple-choice questions (MCQs) are unlikely to be a suitable task for this to take place. Alternatively, an oral presentation may give students the opportunity to explain a key concept as well as allowing students to demonstrate their oral communication skills.

In some units, communication skills may be an essential academic skill distinct from, but related to, the content and context of the unit. Thus, the assessment task outcome should be fairly representative of the curriculum, discipline-specific or essential academic skill outcomes expected of students. The process of matching assessment task outcomes with ILOs ensures reliability. However, even if an assessment task is reliable, it may not be enough to provide a valid measure of student learning.

Valid assessments measure student learning (not something else) and the extent of that learning. There are different types of validity in assessment, including content validity, criterion validity and construct validity. Content validity refers to the extent to which the content of the assessment matches the ILOs. That is, the assessment must be representative of the area of learning being assessed. Assessing content randomly selected from 6 weeks of a 13-week semester in an end-of-semester exam is not representative of, and will not validly measure, a student's overall learning achievement. A student with solid overall knowledge of the entire semester's work can still fail such a narrow exam as adequate opportunity to demonstrate their learning is not possible.

Criterion validity refers to the extent to which the measurement methods are in agreement with external criteria. Examples include alignment of assessment outcomes with course-level learning outcomes, discipline threshold learning outcomes, competency standards and accreditation requirements.

Construct validity, on the other hand, refers to how well an assessment task measures what it claims to measure. If an assessment task is claimed to measure understanding, for example, it should be possible for a student to pass by recalling information. Another example of construct validity is determining the correct challenge level. This translates to how the standard of performance required is articulated, particularly to students.

Here is an example. A group task in a first-year unit may involve students completing a set of learning and assessment activities in an allocated group based on instructions provided by the academic. Assessment could simply look at the quality or product of group work. In the second year, the assessment task design may require students to self-select their group, work collaboratively and demonstrate aspects of teamwork skills, such as communication and negotiation skills. While in the third year, students could be assessed on their capability to collaboratively design and demonstrate leadership in seeing a project to completion. Construct validity is particularly important when designing sequential

32 *Developing assessment methods*

assessment tasks within and across units in a course, as student learning is constructed based on assumed knowledge at each level.

In Chapter 1, we emphasised the importance of achieving internal consistency. From an assessment perspective, the processes for achieving internal consistency should aid our judgements in designing assessments that measure learning and the extent to which learning outcomes are achieved by each student. This not only involves checking the suitability, reliability and validity of assessment tasks, as we explained above. It also means that the method of assessment should yield the same result if it is repeated, or different markers should be able to make the same judgements about a student's achievement of ILOs.

Table 3.1 lists various assessment tasks, a simple definition that explains what the task is, and how it can be utilised in units. However, the task needs to be contextualised to ensure alignment with the unit and the ILOs. The worksheets attached in Appendix D, Tables D1, D2 and D3 will help evaluate the suitability of an assessment task with the action verbs in the unit learning outcomes. There is little benefit in retrofitting a preferred assessment method to the ILOs. Rather, assessment must be reimagined from a learning outcomes perspective (backwards mapping), and designed to enable judgements to be made about what students have learned, to provide clear and useful feedback on their learning, as well as to develop students' own skills for critical judgement and self-direction.

We highly recommend consulting Phil Race's (2014) analysis of various types of assessments. In this analysis, Race considers types of assessment, their "status" – validity, fairness, level of confidence in terms of who completed the task, authenticity, and likely quality of feedback, as well as advantages and disadvantages.

Developing assessment practices that focus students on learning

When designing assessment, it is important to keep in mind that assessment tasks must be realistic, timely and achievable by the student. For example, weekly assessment of learning in a unit may be too much for a student if they are enrolled in fulltime study. Equally, if all the units in a given study period have the same due date for assessment task, students may complain (rightly) about workload issues. Academics may not realise these practical issues when planning assessment, but they need to be dealt with in assessment design. A whole-of-course approach, considering the position and purpose of each unit, is therefore recommended.

Much of the time we see academics combining formative with summative assessments, and usually it is desirable to do so. Diagnostic and formative assessment tasks are primarily used as assessment for learning, and provide feedback on student learning and the effectiveness of teaching. They may not contribute to the student's final grade and/or mark for the unit of study. Summative tasks, on the other hand, are used for the sole purpose of assessment of learning and to grade the student's performance against the unit learning outcomes, and provide a measure of overall achievement. Most commonly, students do not receive feedback on summative tasks.

Table 3.1 Assessment methods for categories of ILOs

Acquisition of knowledge	• Closed-answer tests – Students answer a set of standardised test questions developed by the lecturer. The test may consist of multiple-choice, true/false, matching and sentence-completion items • Formal exams – Students respond to a set of test questions (short, long, essay, multiple choice, problems) developed by the lecturer to describe, explain and present their consolidated understanding of concepts and issues or solve problems • Essays – Students respond in writing to one or more questions or problem situations. They may be asked to compare, discuss, analyse, evaluate, critique and apply their knowledge to describe, explain, argue, synthesise or hypothesise • Oral tests – Students orally respond to a set of questions individually or in groups • Oral presentation – Students give a formal presentation to their peers or select audience on a specific topic area • Self-evaluation forms – Students respond to structured or open-ended questions and describe their learning
Enhancing cognitive skills	• Case studies – Students analyse and give alternative solutions to an event, incident or situation that is problematic. Case study assessment can be administered in oral or written formats and can be either a group or individual exercise • Concept maps – Students make diagrams and drawings that represent thought processes and connections between and among ideas and concepts • Interviews – Students conduct individual or group interviews to demonstrate the ability to source information, collect data, critically analyse and evaluate a particular situation or social issue • Analytic memos/letters – Students write a memo or a letter responding to a real-life problem or issue that demonstrates their analytical abilities for example, work-related issues, community problems
Developing psychomotor skills	• Performance – Students perform a skill, operation or practical task using specified and specialist equipment to demonstrate the ability to perform the task in predictable or unpredictable situations. A clear statement of the required standards of performance should be used and agreed by all parties involved in the assessment process • Observations – Students under the observation of an invigilator/assessor carry out a set of work-based and behavioural tasks to demonstrate the ability to differentiate, apply, detect, operate, structure and perform. Clear standards and performance are set and agreed • Product review – Students develop a product for examination by the lecturer, expert examiner or a panel of examiners. Examples include models, video clip, campaign, website etc.

(Continued)

Table 3.1 (Cont.)

Strengthening problem finding and problem-solving skills	• Documented problem solution – Students document how they have solved a problem individually or as a group in an authentic or simulated context • Audio- and video-taped protocols – Students audio- or video-tape the process of problem-finding or solving situation and present that evidence to substantiate their learning • Reflective journals – Students are required to keep written reflective entries on how they solved/resolved specific problems and the processes they used in problem identification and solving • Computer-based simulations – Students solve problems through computer simulations, coding and decoding, programming, simulating, building models and designing solutions for a range of problems they encounter • Observations – Students are observed by lecturers or expert examiners to ascertain whether useful and appropriate methods are being used strengthen the ability to identify and solve a problem • Oral defence – Students present their problem-finding and problem-solving strategies to peers, a panel of experts or a supervisor to demonstrate their ability to identify, analyse, synthesise, hypothesise and postulate
Changes to attitudes, values and beliefs	• Role playing – Students role play a situation, focusing on attitudes, beliefs, values and feelings. They express their beliefs and feelings, reason their values and attitudes and demonstrate through role play how they defend their position, judge other's positions, advocate, bargain or endorse views • Closed-ended tests – Students answer questions that focus on specific attitudes, beliefs, values and feelings. Although these tests are difficult to construct, they can provide a very useful measure of personality traits and provide useful information as feedback. Care must be taken to ensure validity and reliability of the assessment • Reflective journals – Students document in their journals two types of entries: one that describes an event or situation, and a second that focuses on their feelings and attitudes about that event • Free-form writing – Students respond to a stem sentence or just write about a specific topic. The emphasis is usually on how they feel about a topic, situation or proposition

Adapted from Caffarella (2002).

Most students will not make an effort on work that does not matter in their final result. The challenge, therefore, is to think about ways to make summative assessments more formative and to get students to take formative tests more seriously. This approach is commonly referred to as "scaffolding". Scaffolding involves breaking an assessment task down into stages and requiring students to submit their work to get feedback for learning progressively leading up to final submission.

The issue here from an academic perspective is workload in assessing students' work progressively and providing them with useful feedback on their work. However, from a student perspective, the marks or grades that they receive for summative assessment tasks provide limited information about the quality or their work, and do not indicate how they can improve. While feedback can greatly strengthen learning, it does not necessarily help students develop their own skills for critical judgement and self-direction.

Authentic assessment tasks require students to do things that they would have to do in the real world. Simulation or role play of a scenario, completion of a real-world task, assessment in a workplace setting are all examples of authentic assessment that are useful for improving critical judgement and self-direction of students. Generally, these types of assessment tasks help students contextualise their learning and see how real-life conditions or situations, in all their unpredictability, ambiguity and complexity, affect their theoretical knowledge. Learning is supported and enhanced when students engage in deliberately planned reflective tasks and self and peer assessment activities that require generation and use of feedback for learning.

As students draw their knowledge and skills to engage productively, their behaviour can show the level of capacity and competency they have gained. The controversy about this sort of assessment is centred primarily on its reliability. As highlighted previously, for assessment to be reliable, it should yield the same results if it is repeated. Judgement may also be valid under test circumstances when assessing attitude or ethical behaviour, but does not necessarily predict behaviour in real practice.

Many university degree courses promote and claim to develop graduates who are capable of monitoring their own performance and that of their peers. However, in reality, students may not develop the capacity to adequately or accurately evaluate their own learning or that of their peers unless they are taught how to do so. Some academics involve students in the assessment process and are consciously attempting to develop those metacognitive self-management skills to help students to learn to live together – carrying out joint projects, or learning to manage conflicts – as we highlighted in Chapter 2, its importance and spirit of respect for the values of pluralism, mutual understand and peace.

Nevertheless, as assessment serves many needs, including those of students, teachers, the institution and the community, we are obligated to continue assessing and grading students' work. Nightingale et al. (1996) summarised the needs of various stakeholders in the assessment process as indicated below in Table 3.2.

36 *Developing assessment methods*

Table 3.2 Purpose of assessment and challenges they present to stakeholders

Stakeholders	May need to know:	Motivations and priorities
Students	• How they are doing in general • Whether they are reaching a required standard • If they will have something to show to others	• Am I on track? • Will I pass or graduate? • Please employ me, give me a scholarship
Teachers	• Whether students are achieving the ILOs • Whether they can certify that students can proceed to other units for which theirs may be a prerequisite • If they will have evidence to show to others that their students are successful	• Am I getting through, are they doing their work? • A student who passes my unit should be able to cope with yours • Please consider me for a position or promotion
Institution	• Whether students are achieving ILOs at course level • If they will have evidence to prove to others that their graduates have achieved what the institution claims they have achieved • Whether they can certify that students can proceed to employment, professional practice or further study • Whether they can accept applicants into programs of study	• Are our units effective, are our staff effective? • Please continue to fund us or support us • Our graduates meet your requirements • Do you have the required pre-requisite knowledge? What is your level of achievement compared to other applicants?
Community	• Whether the institution and the teachers are effective • Whether the individuals that graduate are employable or have the capability to practice, etc.	• We will continue to support you or fund you • You may work here, you may teach here, or you may practice as a doctor or a nurse here

For obvious reasons, conflicts of interest are inherent in the needs of various stakeholders; these conflicts lead to some of the major issues in assessment. Issues could include:

- authenticating the student in online assessments;
- assessing higher-order learning using online assessments;
- assessing student learning in large classes;
- minimising plagiarism, collusion and contract cheating;
- assessing group work;

Developing assessment methods 37

- assessing the individual's collaborative effort, contributions and performance in team work; and/or
- assessing students who are unfamiliar with assessment practices in a Higher Education context.

First-year assessment principles

Until now, we have not addressed the issue of students' *assessment literacy*. This is a term used by Race (2014) to describe the level and types of "know-how" students have as they face assessment tasks. He notes that assessment practices at university are not necessarily like those at secondary school, so unit designers need to take this into account as they consider how they measure achievement of learning outcomes, provide feedback and design learning activities aligned with specific tasks. Development of students' assessment literacy covers five things, according to Race:

1   Ability to tackle a variety of task types;
2   Knowing how to go about completing assessment tasks strategically (in terms of planning, time management, and the like);
3   Being able to figure out exactly what a task is asking and what the output might be (interpreting instructions and rubrics);
4   Becoming familiar with grading systems; and
5   Successfully navigating electronic completion and submission systems.

Further, studies into the first-year experience have shown that specific learning and learner needs should be considered in both unit design and execution. In particular, we point to Sally Kift and colleagues' work on "Transition pedagogy" (2010) which highlighted assessment as one of the six principles of first-year curriculum design. In particular, the following assessment practice principles provides guidance for educators to tackle a critical question – *'how do we design assessment in first year units to maximise students chances of success in later years?'*

- Ensure assessment is at the heart of the developing learning experiences;
- Set appropriate levels (or expectations);
- Provide early, low-stakes assessment to ease students in;
- Unpack the mysteries of university assessment (see "assessment literacy" above);
- Provide opportunities for self and peer assessment; and
- Emphasise feed-*forward* (Chapter 5).

Upholding values, standards and integrity of learning

Notwithstanding the issues and challenges with assessment, the central concern for assessment design is to ensure academic standards and integrity. Integrity

38 *Developing assessment methods*

simply means upholding fundamental values including honestly, trust, fairness, respect and responsibility. Irrespective of the type of assessment task – diagnostic, formative or summative – staff and students are expected to adhere to these values.

One way of ensuring that these values are upheld consistently is to plan for working collaboratively with the unit team (including casual/sessional academic staff) and/or the members of the assessment panel appointed for each unit. The team or the panel should work toward designing, developing and reviewing each of the assessment tasks in the unit, including the rubrics or marking scheme provided to students, to generate a shared understanding of the expectations and standards required for completing each of the assessment tasks. This would also aid in developing strategies that ensure comparability of performance by students enrolled within a unit, assessing to the same standard, so that learning is measured against a set of criteria and standards rather than against a supposed norm. Some of the strategies that could be planned in the assessment design process include double marking, blind marking, panel marking and objective test questionnaires.

Norm-referenced assessment uses the achievement of a group of students to set the standards for specific grades or simply for passing or failing. The best $x\%$ of students get the best result, the worst $x\%$ fail. Grading on the curve is an example of norm-referencing, but this approach to assessment is no longer recommended in Australian universities, as it does not support reliable and valid ways of measuring student attainment of ILOs.

Criterion-referenced assessment establishes standards for specific grades, and/or for passing or failing. A student who meets the criteria gets the specified result. Some disciplines of study will have professional competency standards that students have to meet for graduation. Those disciplines will expect students to perform certain functions as a result of their knowledge, skills and attitudes. Competence is developed by education, training and experience. Assurance of learning tends to be premised on a compensatory approach where good performance in one summative assessment task can be used to compensate for poor performance in the other summative assessment tasks within a unit.

Summary

When designing assessment tasks, ensure that the method of assessment is consistent with the ILO(s) being assessed. Assessment methods chosen must allow for reasonable judgements to be made that confirm the extent to which the student has achieved the ILOs. The assessment method chosen must also support and assess real learning. The assessment workload for both students and markers should be reasonable.

Efficiencies should be achieved in the way we describe each assessment activity to students through unit guides and during classes: explicitly stating the purpose of the assessment activity, what students are expected to know, do and demonstrate in order to successfully complete required task(s). If you find that a particular outcome is not being assessed at all because it does not align with any of the assessment tasks, then consider the usefulness of that outcome, as well as the method of assessment.

At the very least, the method of assessment should elicit specific learning of the outcome intended, and measure precisely that outcome. Assessment designs must:

- ensure that students have evidence of their achievement against each of the ILOs;
- ensure that student learning of ILOs is scaffolded and that the task allows students to acquire, practise and demonstrate learning intended;
- include an appropriate mix of authentic tasks that promotes reflection, self and peer assessment to develop student readiness for employability.

Rubrics should be used, wherever possible not only as a feed-forward mechanism to improve student understanding of the task(s) and expected level of performance, but also to grade their performance and provide feedback to support their learning. The next chapter provides detail on the use of rubrics as part of the assessment process.

References

Biggs, J.B. & Tang, C.S.-K. 2011. *Teaching for Quality Learning at University: What the student does*, 4th edn, The Society for Research into Higher Education (SRHE) and Open University Press, Maidenhead, Berkshire.

Boud, D. & Associates 2010, *Assessment 2020: Seven propositions for assessment reform in higher education*, Australian Learning and Teaching Council, Sydney, Australia.

Caffarella, R.S. 2002, *Planning Programs for Adult Learners: A practical guide for educators, trainers and staff developers*, 2nd edn, vol. 1, Jossey-Bass, New York.

Kift, S.M., Nelson, K.J. & Clarke, J.A. 2010, 'Transition pedagogy: a third generation approach to FYE: a case study of policy and practice for the higher education sector', *International Journal of the First Year in Higher Education*, vol. 1, no. 1, 1–20. Retrieved from https://eprints.qut.edu.au/33635/1/c33635.pdf

Nightingale, P., Wiata, I.T., Toohey, S., Ryan, G., Hughes, C. & Magin, D. 1996, *Assessing Learning in Universities*, UNSW Press, Sydney, Australia.

Race, P. 2014, *Making Learning Happen: A guide for post-compulsory education*, 3rd edn, Sage, London.

4 Designing rubrics for enhancing student learning

Introduction

Good course and unit design processes continuously and consciously maintain sight of the desired quality of student work. After all, high-quality student learning is the reason we put effort into unit design or redesign. Rubrics precisely spell out the criteria and standards by which students' work is to be judged. The word "rubric" is derived from the Latin "ruber", meaning "red", and relating to heading or directions provided. It is an evaluation tool that helps academics make objective judgements about the quality of student activity and learning, and enables them to provide structured feedback to connect their performance with the learning outcomes intended for their achievement. Fundamentally, the assessment task design process is incomplete without clear articulation of the quality and performance expected from students.

The need for rubrics

Consider the assessment task which is nothing more than: "Outline and discuss the Marxist tradition of social theory. What is the legacy of this tradition for sociology?" As we discussed in Chapter 3, a teacher's intention may be that a broad question like this would allow for a range of responses from students (creativity, perhaps), and so the teacher might be reluctant to give more detail. However, the question itself does not convey any insight to the student or to the teacher/assessor about the quality of the response required or their activity in terms of conducting search, performing analysis of different viewpoints or forming their own viewpoint when compared to that of others. Providing no "rubric" commonly results in students feeling confused about what the assessor is expecting of them, or students working towards producing something they think is required only to receive feedback that it was not. In both cases both the teacher/assessor and the student can come away disappointed by the teaching–learning experience.

Characteristics of an effective rubric

We often see marking rubrics that are developed to prioritise formatting and structuring details over details about the quality of work expected. Such marking guides might specify:

- font and margin sizes;
- the number of references to be used (without specification as to their quality); or
- the organisation of the document in a particular fashion.

These may be genuinely important considerations for a given task and/or discipline, but in most they convey little to do with the quality of a response and are possibly best described as assessment instructions. Many submissions might be excellent in terms of quality, but lack in terms of the specifications above. Take the example that a student might submit extremely well-researched work that is poorly formatted. Is it fair to penalise their work based on how it is set out? A unit designer will need to ask if these aspects are truly relevant reasons for deducting marks by paying close attention to the unit ILOs.

Bookhart and Nitko (2008) recommend that rubrics should be designed based on whether the assessment criteria are considered separately or together, and whether the rubric is general enough to be associated with a number of assessment tasks or if the association is specific to an assessment task. We argue that thoughtfully developed rubrics define and describe our expectations of student activity and have at least the following five essential design characteristics, making them worth the time investing into developing them. Rubrics:

1 Define the quality and features of work.
2 Guide students and teachers through the learning and assessment process.
3 Grade the quality of student activity in the unit and their performance.
4 Provide feedback to students (with a focus on quality and performance improvements).
5 Validate the consistency of academic judgement to ensure effective learning.

Defining the quality and performance of student work

Without explicit criteria for completing the assessment task it is probable that many students will put a great deal of effort into something teachers do not expect or want to receive. This is problematic from the point of view of both the students and teachers/assessors. Students, on the one hand, would be rightly frustrated by the confusion, and without explicit criteria, assessors will need to put a lot of effort into giving individual students feedback by explaining why the work they received is not what they expected. Moreover, the time taken to grade and give feedback to students can become extended beyond what is expected (or paid) as assessors consider the range of quality of

42 *Designing rubrics*

students' work and consider their relative merit. Simply put, more explicitness will result in delivering to students the clarity of learning intended, teachers and assessors receiving what they want to mark, and an increase time efficiency for all.

Clarification of expectations can take place in classes or via online communication, but we advise that simply having a discussion with students about the quality of work does not do away with the need for a rubric because these discussions rely on students' interpretation and this might result in an inaccurate interpretation of what is required. That is not to say that discussion about the quality/features of the work is not important: it is. However, a structured rubric will provide the framework for any discussion and ensure that all parties can evaluate assessable work using the same parameters. As such, rubrics should be seen as a natural part and parcel of the assessment. An assessment task should never be delivered to students without a rubric that clearly stipulates the outcomes expected (criteria) or without specifying the quality features of the product of their learning and performance requirements through their activity (minimum standard).

Guiding teachers and students through the teaching/learning process

Once developed, a rubric will act as a guide or compass for teaching and learning, bringing to the fore a detailed vision for student success. A rubric can serve as a tool for conversation about learning and performance expectations, as it provides a platform for negotiation between the teacher and the students in planning their activity. It is common to discuss the qualities and features of submitted work at the time of handing out a task. This strategy or concept, which stems from the work of Hattie and Timperley (2007), is called *feed up*. We discuss this in more detail in the next chapter. Essentially, this term refers to providing students with clarity about where they are headed with their learning, as opposed to *feedback*, which is provided during or after their activity, or *feed forward*, which is provided to students after marking or grading their assessment task submission. In other words, rubrics have an instructional role (for more on this, see Andrade 2000).

All teachers wish to receive good-quality work from students, but much of the work of an assessment task is done outside of the direct supervision. For assessments that are completed by students outside of "class" time, the accompanying rubric needs to be one that provides this explicit detail, and to be something that allows for students to self-check as they are completing the task. We consider the development of students' metacognition in more detail in Chapter 6: self-checking or student judgement of the quality of their own work or performance in an activity is an important part of the metacognitive processes that aid learning. This is frequently referred to as reflection in the higher-education context, and is promoted to empower students to become reflective practitioners and life-long learners.

Designing rubrics   43

Grading

One important and obvious benefit of constructing a rigorous rubric is to make grading more effective. Developing a rubric is an important process in assessment validity and reliability. As discussed in the previous chapter, a valid assessment is one that measures what it is intended to measure as articulated in the unit learning outcomes. A reliable assessment is one that produces consistency of judgement. A good-quality rubric plays a significant role in maximising both of these features: defining the quality features, or criteria, of the work to be produced is likely to tighten alignment between the task and the learning outcomes, while defining the standards of measurement will work towards producing consistent judgement between markers and consistent work quality between groups.

Providing feedback to students

A good rubric provides text that articulates feedback to students about the quality of their work in advance (feed up). In terms of feedback, use of a well-designed rubric will communicate feedback to students about the evaluation of their submitted work, and the grade, without having to take the time to provide wholly unique responses. For those who use recorded verbal feedback, the rubric will provide a useful focus and script.

Evaluating teaching and curriculum design

Finally, using rubrics can highlight aspects of the unit design and/or delivery that need attention. Keeping records of how students' work compares with the rubric will inform curriculum design and delivery for the next offering of the unit. Although we will discuss this in more detail later in this book, an example is the use of LMS-embedded rubric functions that allow for collation of grade standards per criterion for the purpose of overall review and evaluation.

Practical strategies for developing an effective rubric

Structuring a rubric from scratch

Constructing an effective rubric literally starts with a simple table, and generally speaking, a rubric will look something like Table 4.1.

It is a matter of preference that some unit designers prefer to have higher standards to the right-hand side of the table. There will also be variations in the number of standards according to the nature and context of the specific assessment activity (for example, the number of marks associated with it) and a university or department's grading policy. Generally, we recommend that the number of standards are kept to a minimum, depending on the spread of marks. In Table 4.2, there are four descriptors applied to work including and above a "pass" level,

44 Designing rubrics

Table 4.1 The structure of a rubric

	Highest standard	Intermediate standard 2	Intermediate standard 1	Pass standard	Fail standard
Criterion 1 and explanation of criterion, and marks available	Descriptor	Descriptor	Descriptor	Descriptor	Descriptor
	Mark or mark range	Mark or mark range	Mark or mark range	Mark or mark range (minimum is pass)	Mark or mark range
Criterion 2 and explanation of criterion, and marks available	Descriptor	Descriptor	Descriptor	Descriptor	Descriptor
	Mark or mark range	Mark or mark range	Mark or mark range	Mark or mark range (minimum is pass)	Mark or mark range
Etc.					

Table 4.2 Too many standards

Unacceptable work	Fair work	Good work	Very good work	Excellent work
0–2.45	2.5–3.2	3.25–3.7	3.75–4.2	4.25–5

Table 4.3 Fewer standards

Standard 1	Standard 2	Standard 3
0–1.5	2–3	3.5–4

meaning the unit designer needed to create five descriptors for each criterion worth five marks each. The resulting differentiation of mark allocation between and within each standard was negligible – in 0.05 mark increments – over a 100-mark unit, and created unnecessary work.

Table 4.3 shows how criteria attracting fewer marks can be addressed using fewer standards with a reasonable degree of accuracy – in this case 0.5 marks for a 100-mark unit. If a criterion for the same task requires a greater range of marks, an extra column may be added for that one criterion alone (in other words, one does not need the exact same number of standards for each criterion).

Naming the standards is also something for consideration. Note that the column names in Table 4.2 are *evaluative terms*, designed to provide a measure of feedback in and of themselves to students. The column names in Table 4.3 simply delineate standards of work and rely on the descriptors to communicate guidance and feedback. We tend to recommend the latter

Designing rubrics 45

rather than the former for the very reason that these evaluative remarks can be misleading for students to understanding the *qualities* of their work, as well as the fact that a different number of standards may be required for different criteria.

Deciding on the type of rubric you need

We know that it is commonplace to seek rubric samples online or to start with existing ones when redesigning a unit. However, unit designers need to remember to *critically examine* them for quality; there are good and bad examples, and much in-between. Developing a good-quality rubric requires delineating important criteria for assessment. When unit designers seek our advice for designing a rubric that measures student performance in an assessment task, a key question we ask them to consider is: What evidence is required to convince you of good-quality learning and student performance against the unit ILOs?

Usually it is easy to define evidence needed for good-quality student *performance* for assessment, but not good-quality *learning*. Good-quality student performance is expressed in terms of their action (for example, conduct an experiment), the processes that have applied for completing the activity (for example, their experimental design), and the product of their learning (for example, their observations, analysis and the results of their experiment submitted for assessment in the form of written reports and calculations). Performance standards associated with grade levels can be developed to define the quality of outcome expected from student activity in each dimension (action, process, product).

Such a rubric is often referred to as *analytical* rubric, which outlines the criteria that will be used for assessing the structure and quality of the documentation (product) that they submit for assessment following their activity. Analytical rubrics can be task-specific or generic. A *task-specific rubric* is specific to the assessment task it is associated with and is usually not useful for assessing overall student performance. Generally, task-specific rubrics attract binary feedback, for example whether a student was successful in measuring temperature changes or not, or whether a student was able to execute a program on a microprocessor to make it function as a timer or not. Sometimes, task-specific rubrics list the structure that students should have applied for constructing a report or an essay, or specify the theories that must be applied in their analysis, etc.

Generic rubrics use criteria and standards that can be used to generalise student performance across a number of tasks. However, the tasks have to be instances of the same learning outcome or transferable skill, for example, critical thinking and teamwork skills. Generic rubrics provide after-the-fact information about the quality of work that is expected from a whole family of tasks unless a student is able to thoroughly comprehend, envision and execute criteria like "well-written argument", "thorough analysis" or "ability to solve problems" in light of the task at hand. Given that it is unlikely that most students will be able unpack this for themselves, it is up to teachers to provide clarification, and this clarification needs to be provided with specificity on a task-by-task basis.

46   *Designing rubrics*

Analytical rubrics often fall short of explaining the outcome of student activity in relation to the ILOs assessed, unless the stated unit ILOs are: develop an experimental design; conduct an experiment; and submit a report with observations, analysis and results. That is, it does not provide the student enough information about the evidence that is necessary to convince that their learning of content or accumulation of skills through the completion of various parts has contributed to the higher purpose, which is enhanced learning or achievement of unit ILOs.

In Australian universities, students are generally assessed using multiple summative assessment tasks within a unit, with the final mark calculated based on aggregating marks obtained across these summative assessment tasks. So, the assurance of student learning where good performance in one summative assessment task compensates for poor performance in another within a unit, weakens the overall purpose of assessment for learning (Sadler 1986). This requires marking rubrics to be designed to provide an indication of overall quality standard required to demonstrate achievement of the ILOs.

Such rubrics are called *holistic* rubrics. Holistic rubrics have a higher purpose, which requires students to see the big picture rather than just the atomistic parts. They guide students to develop the capacity to evaluate and judge their own performance, and require the assessor to also think about the greater purpose of the assessment for and assessment of student learning (Ajjawi et al. 2018).

In higher education, there is also a tendency to mix both analytical criteria and holistic criteria to focus on the detail and at the same time connect the big picture to the students. Such rubrics are called hybrid rubrics. In *hybrid* rubrics, ILOs associated with the assessment task can be used as final criteria or hurdle requirement. This can help identify any misconceptions or gaps in student learning and ensure that students do not progress to the next phase of their study, even if they satisfy the minimum standard required from the atomistic parts. Thus, the holistic criteria in the hybrid rubric can be used as a hurdle requirement to require students to prepare and provide evidence to convince that their learning of content or accumulation of skills through the completion of various assessment tasks has contributed to the higher strategic purpose envisioned for the unit within and beyond the course.

Evaluating a new or existing rubric

A set of assessment criteria and the associated standards make up a rubric. Assessment criteria in a rubric should align closely with the unit ILOs, depending on the unit itself. They can be the same as, or sub-criteria of those ILOs. A well-designed rubric conveys learning expectations to all who may be teaching into a unit and help them plan teaching/learning activities. Rubrics aid grading reliability and consistency in matching student performance in a specific learning or assessment activity, even when different assessors or markers are involved in the process of evaluating student learning. Like any other evaluation tool, marking rubrics are contextual to the assessment task and therefore we do not recommend using a rubric that was created for a different assessment context or a different purpose without fully understanding its design intent.

The following five considerations will help unit designers to consider the essential features of their rubric and decide whether and how an existing rubric might need improvement. The same criteria will help unit designers to design a rubric from scratch:

1   alignment with the task, and course and unit learning outcomes;
2   distinctness of descriptors;
3   clarity and succinctness of descriptors;
4   reasonableness of expectations;
5   appropriateness of level of standards.

Alignment with the task, and course and unit learning outcomes

First and foremost, we seek *validity* in a rubric. Essentially, that means that it is closely aligned with the question or problem posed as well as the unit outcomes. We want it to measure what it is intended to measure. It is unfortunately common to find that a task description requires a feature or quality that is not − or not obviously − included in the rubric, or vice versa. It is not that unit designers intend for this to be the case; this could be the result of overlooking detail, or even the result of continuous improvement in one area of the unit or other, or changeover of unit coordinators.

To evaluate alignment, a close *mapping* examination of the ILOs, assessment tasks and the criteria needs to be carried out. Recall from earlier chapters that when we talk about alignment in unit deign, we are essentially talking about ensuring that aspects of the unit match, and mapping is simply the process of doing this. Alignment will depend on how well the tasks are designed to address unit ILOs and how well the criteria are suited to those. We do not recommend using the same rubric for multiple tasks unless the tasks are essentially the same. There may, however, be a general format that suits the discipline and the qualities/features unit and course designers are looking for in work. In fact, this is recommended for the sake of consistency and alignment between units.

Here are initial questions you might ask as you examine an existing rubric or a draft:

- Would you be awarding grades to qualities and/or features that are not a requirement for achieving the learning outcomes?
- Do the learning outcomes require qualities or features that are not contained in the rubric?

Distinctness and consistency of descriptors

Both validity and reliability of assessment rest on a rubric that ensures students' work cannot be described by more than one descriptor. Each descriptor needs to

48 *Designing rubrics*

be distinct and definite, and have consistent reference to the same qualities/features (including the nomenclature) needs to be made across standards for each criterion. Indistinct descriptors are not only a problem for one assessor; they become more of a problem for more than one assessor in terms of coming to an agreement about the features and standards of students' work.

Clarity and succinctness

One of the questions that unit designers have raised with us is about the balance between providing a rubric with too few or too many words. In an attempt to be accurate, many rubric writers can tend to produce lengthy, detailed descriptors. There are two problems with this: the first is that students may decide not to read them closely; the second is that the detail can be too restrictive for some types of assessments.

This might at first seem at odds with the "distinct and definite" criterion above, but it is not. When students submit work that a teacher/assessor has not imagined, an inflexible rubric will result in "fudging" the grade to fit and result in a loss of validity and reliability. Moreover, lengthy and detailed descriptors can simply be counterproductive. Exercise strict analysis of wording to provide succinct descriptors that are easy to read, understand and apply. This is a matter of semantics. Some questions you might ask include:

- Is the rubric too lengthy and therefore off-putting to students?
- Can the descriptors be written using more succinct language?
- Are the descriptors too precise or detailed to match the variety of work – strengths or weaknesses – to be submitted by students?
- Are the descriptors written in plain English and grammatically correct?

Reasonableness

Each of the criteria and standards must be "reasonable". This is a fairly fluid judgement, so when examining an existing rubric or providing a review for a colleague, consciously consider whether the students might be spending too little or too much effort on particular aspects of the task. A rubric should reflect an appropriate level of expectation placed upon the students at each described standard. The lowest "pass" standard should be a threshold that reflects "adequate" work, and anything of lesser quality will reflect inadequate work to deem the student as having met the outcome. The highest standard should be attainable by the best, or near best, work. It is common to find the highest standard describing "over and above" the requirements of the task, however this should not be case for standards- or criterion-referenced assessment. Similarly, the higher standards should present some challenge for students, indicative of their learning in the unit, yet

Designing rubrics 49

not ask for the deployment of academic skills and application of background knowledge the students may not have developed.

Consider also whether or not the requirements of the rubric reflect the level of the students. For instance, we have seen rubrics intended for first year students which are pitched far above what might expected at this level. On the other hand, we have also seen rubrics intended for capstone units which require relatively little effort or quality of work in light of the advanced status of the students. Another aspect to consider regarding reasonableness is the weighting of each criterion. Although it may be simpler to give each criterion the same weighting, this could result in an imbalance with respect to time and effort and/or relative importance.

Table 4.4 provides some ideas for the highest standard and the next-to-highest standard. We do not expect this to be suitable for all assessment types, or disciplines, but it shows the difference between one standard and the next. We recommend consulting the SOLO Taxonomy (Biggs & Collis 1982) and/ or Anderson and Krathwohl's (2001) Revised Bloom's Taxonomy to construct the standards.

Summary

There are many guides available for writing rubrics, and they are largely similar. The worksheet that we have developed (see Appendix E) over time as we have worked with academics across a range of disciplines, helps you evaluate the quality of criteria and standards used in rubrics. We recommend it as stable and applicable across disciplines. We also recommend the following *seven steps* for creating an effective rubric:

1   Write down the content that needs to be covered in the students' work (what needs to be included).
2   Decide on the must-have features and qualities of the students' work.
3   Group the must-have features into several criteria, and give them relative weightings (consult graduate, course and unit learning outcomes).
4   Decide on your standards (labelling, mark allocation).
5   Write the top-most standard descriptor for each criterion, using your notes at 2 and 3 above (note that specific content does not have to be included in the descriptor, but reference to it does). This describes the work you really want to mark. Be careful about your wording. Bloom's Taxonomy and SOLO Taxonomy will come in helpful here.
6   Write the descriptors for a fail grade for each criterion, as well as the passing (threshold) level. This represents the point at which students are deemed to have met the outcomes.
7   Write the descriptors of the standards below the top-most, stating what the shortcomings were. These should be relatively minor compared with the next level down.

50 Designing rubrics

Table 4.4 Ideas for highest and next-to-highest standards

Category of criteria type	Top level (Excellent)	Next to top level (Very good)
Quality of analysis	• The analysis is detailed	• Some minor details are missing, *or* there are a few areas of superficiality
	• The analysis is comprehensive	• Some minor limitations in terms of scope
	• All analysis is relevant	• Some minor areas of relevance left unaddressed, *or* some analysis is irrelevant
	• Analysis addresses complexities in …	• Some complexity is addressed or alluded to, but is not fully examined
	• The analysis provides original insights	• Most of the analysis is original; there is some reliance on the analysis of others
	• All claims are substantiated	• Several claims remain unsubstantiated
	• Relevant literature is applied consistently and accurately to support claims	• One or two sources of literature are not relevant or have weak connection to the work
Depth of understanding	• All justifications are reasonable, *or* all arguments are rational	• There are several minor flaws in logic, *or* it remains unconvincing
	• Key concepts are described/ applied correctly	• There are some minor inaccuracies in the description/ application of key concepts
	• Key ideas and concepts are synthesised to develop a coherent argument	• A few minor disconnections between parts of the work
Quality of communication	• Specified referencing conventions are applied correctly throughout	• Several minor errors in referencing conventions
	• The work is logically structured and coherent	• One or two aspects of the task seem out of place
	• Appropriate academic language is used throughout	• There are a few areas where language used is not of the appropriate academic tone
	• The work contains few or no grammatical errors	• The work contains a few minor grammatical errors

References

Ajjawi, R., Tai, J., Dawson, P. & Boud, D. 2018, 'Conceptualising Evaluative Judgement for sustainable assessment in higher education', in D. Boud, R. Ajjawi, P. Dawson & J. Tai (eds), *Developing Evaluative Judgement in Higher Education*, 1st edn, Routledge, Abingdon.

Anderson, L. & Krathwohl, D. 2001, *A Taxonomy for Learning, Teaching and Assessing: A revision of Bloom's taxonomy of educational objectives*, Longman, New York.

Andrade, H.G. 2000, 'Using rubrics to promote thinking and learning'. *Educational leadership*, vol. 57, no. 5, pp. 13–19.

Biggs, J.B. & Collis, K.F. 1982, *Evaluating the Quality of Learning: The SOLO taxonomy*, Academic Press, New York.

Bookhart, S. & Nitko, A. 2008, *How to Create and Use Rubrics for Formative Assessment and Grading*, Pearson Education, Upper Saddle River, NJ.

Hattie, J. & Timperley, H. 2007, 'The power of feedback', *Review of Educational Research*, vol. 77, no. 1, pp. 81–112.

Sadler, R. 1986, 'Discussion Paper 4. Defining achievement levels', at http://hdl.handle.net/11343/115859.

5 Devising an overall strategy for providing feedback

Introduction

Feedback is an essential part of the teaching–learning nexus that is often overlooked as an essential part of unit design from the outset. Feedback provides the basis for a reciprocal relationship between teacher/assessor and student, in addition to that which is created in a physical classroom. It provides significant teaching and learning opportunities at key points during a teaching period, especially where assessment is formative in nature (Chapter 3). In the case of some online units, feedback may be the only planned communication between teacher/assessor and students. Its significance cannot be played down.

John Hattie (2009) is best known for examining a large body of data about the effects of various practices and conditions on learning, and argues that feedback is "among the most powerful influences on achievement" (p. 173). Hattie's data analysis informs us that "some types of feedback are more powerful than others" (p. 174), highlighting an important point: simply giving feedback does not necessarily mean that it will assist students' learning. Most university teachers and assessors are aware of this and frequently remark that time spent providing feedback has been wasted. Why is this the case? Commonly, students:

- do not read feedback;
- read feedback but do not understand it;
- read feedback but misunderstand it;
- read feedback and contest it; or
- actively ignore feedback.

Sometimes it is not possible to know which of these is the issue. Our aim is thus to diminish the possibility of each occurring. We want to make students' real *engagement* with the feedback they receive our main aim, and to do this we need to plan for that engagement in the unit design process.

Effective feedback

Nicol and MacFarlane-Dick (2006, p. 205) list and explain the seven principles of *effective* feedback. They claim that good feedback practice:

1　helps clarify what good performance is (goals, criteria, expected standards);
2　facilitates the development of self-assessment (reflection) in learning;
3　delivers high quality information to students about their learning;
4　encourages teacher and peer dialogue around learning;
5　encourages positive motivational beliefs and self-esteem;
6　provides opportunities to close the gap between current and desired performance; and
7　provides information to teachers that can be used to help shape their teaching.

This list can challenge teachers'/assessors' timeworn views of feedback as simply letting students know what they did wrong in the past so as not to do these things again in the future. Among other things, this list highlights the power feedback has in the actual *learning* process as a *relationship* between teacher and students. Clearly, if students do not engage with feedback, it cannot be effective in these ways.

Planning feedback

Unit designers and coordinators need to consider the effectiveness of feedback, but they also have efficiencies to consider. One of the most common complaints of teachers/assessors is the time that is spent giving feedback to students with little apparent gain. In some cases, as a response, assessors have reduced the amount of feedback they have given by employing certain practices like only providing feedback when a student requests it. This is one option, but we do not support this generally, unless the feedback is likely to be unhelpful for future study. It is also common practice to not provide feedback on final examination scripts. Putting aside these exceptions, we support the development of a strategy to maximise the power of feedback whilst minimising the time and effort required to give it.

Developing good quality rubrics (see Chapter 4) will help to balance effectiveness and efficiency, but they should be part of a more holistic, integrated approach that supports teaching and learning at all times. Race (2002) offers a set of attributes or qualities for providing feedback to do just this. He says that feedback should be: timely; intimate and individual; empowering; providing opportunities; and manageable. Students are working and learning throughout the teaching term, but if only two or three tasks make up the assessment for the unit, they may only have two or three opportunities to receive significant feedback on their work (even fewer, perhaps, if the final task is a summative examination). The question is, how do we design a unit so that we can achieve all this? Give students opportunities to receive feedback on their work throughout the unit by building these into the unit teaching and learning activities.

54　*Devising an overall strategy for feedback*

Strategies for engaging students

A research study carried out by Weaver (2006) found that students were often disengaged from feedback "because either the feedback does not contain enough to guide or motivate students, or they have insufficient understanding of academic discourse to interpret comments accurately" (pp. 391–392). Making feedback more attractive to students may rely on only a few techniques (see Race's attributes above).

We agree with Gibbs (2015) and others that timing is of the essence with feedback. For students, receiving feedback weeks after they have submitted their work can be too late either because they have already put time and effort into completing the following task, or because the work is out of mind. Simply, students may not have the time to engage with "reliving" their work. The more time has passed, the more cognitive and temporal effort this will take.

It can be the case that students receive feedback that is not closely aligned with the task requirements and learning outcomes of the unit. This simply means that the feedback is not relevant. Student respondents of Weaver's (2006) study found that feedback that was unrelated to assessment criteria was unhelpful. If students do perceive this feedback to be irrelevant, it is likely that the task description/ and/or rubrics need to be adjusted.

Feedback also needs to be relevant to the students and the unit they are undertaking. Providing feedback that extends beyond what is required of a student in a given unit, for example, may not be relevant, and therefore contributes to the teaching academic's time and effort, and increases the likelihood that students will not engage with the feedback. All these things will help to maximise students' use of feedback that you give to them, and the effect it has on the improvement of their work.

Feed up, feedback and feed forward

The three concepts of *feed up, feedback* and *feed forward* are proposed by the feedback model of Hattie and Timperley (2007). In this model, effective feedback answers three questions – "Where am I going?", "How am I doing?" and "Where to next?" – respectively addressing "feed up, feed back [sic] and feed forward" (p. 88). Further, Beaumont, O'Doherty and Shannon (2011) developed what they call the *dialogic feedback cycle*, a model that considers feedback as a reiterative movement through a cyclical process of pre-, during- and post-task instruction. Sadler (1989) said:

> the learner has to (a) possess a concept of the *standard* … being aimed for, (b) compare the *actual* (or current) *level of performance* with the standard, and (c) engage in appropriate *action* which leads to some closure of the gap [between].
>
> (p. 121)

Devising an overall strategy for feedback   55

From our perspective, this is how the effectiveness–efficiency balance occurs, with careful planning of this triumvirate as a forward-focused process embedded into the design of the unit. Below are some practical activities that can be embedded into the unit design, as part of the scheduled learning activities.

Practical pre-submission activities: for providing feed up and feedback

Put simply, receiving higher-quality submissions from students will facilitate the feedback process by making it a much more efficient and enjoyable teaching experience. It is worth the time and effort to ensure students have an accurate idea of what you are after from the outset, and this is why rubrics have such an important role. The activities outlined on the following pages can be used prior to the submission of the task to allow for true formative practices discussed by both Hattie and Timperley (2007); and Sadler (1989) and Beaumont et al. (2011). Give serious consideration to embedding activities like these into your unit at the design stage to set goals for student learning (feed up) and to indicate how they are performing (feedback).

1 Rubric deconstruction

It is unwise to make the assumption that students will read a rubric and immediately understand how to meet its requirements, even if there has been a great deal of care given to its development. Plan an activity to take students through a thorough deconstruction, explaining words and illustrating what is meant by specific aspects of the rubric. Allow students to clarify their understanding by asking questions such as, "What happens if I … ?" and, "Is [example] what you are after?". Please see Chapter 4 for advice about how to avoid ambiguity and confusion, and note that considering rubrics as instructional devices will mean more clarity for students.

If you are using a grid rubric with criteria and standards, the first step is to explain the criteria against which the students' work will be assessed. What are the qualities of work you are looking for? This will focus the students on the important aspects of the task, ensuring that they do not spend time on unimportant things. Because students tend to learn better when *actively* engaged, an approach that avoids the teacher/assessor merely expressing, even with elaboration, is less likely to impact on students' understanding than an approach that requires them to constructively work on developing a shared understanding. It is also through this process that weaknesses in the expression of the criteria can be discovered and amended. (See Chapter 4 for advice about how to avoid ambiguity.)

2 Sample marking

A particularly useful strategy to provide feed up is to provide students with several *varying* samples of work from a previous cohort and work with the

56 *Devising an overall strategy for feedback*

students to mark them using the rubric. If there is no access to previous samples, it is worth investing some time in creating at least one to use for the activity. In fact, needing to develop one's own sample can highlight minor issues related to the task for teachers/assessors because issues with wording or rubric design can reveal themselves only when teachers/assessors put themselves in the place of students. For students, sample marking will shine light on what they should do or avoid doing, but this will only happen as long as the instruction that accompanies it is clearly focused on analysis and evaluation of the sample.

There are several benefits of using pre-prepared samples. The first is that it puts the personal aside, and allows for objective measurement. Students can be far more open to and comfortable with critiquing the work of someone they do not know. The second is that teachers/assessors will not need to rely on students having completed a draft of their work, as with self-marking (below). Finally, it allows teachers/assessors to be in control of the exercise through already having analysed the work. The only difficulty they may find with this is finding a sample that demonstrates the kinds of strengths and weaknesses in student work that you would like to bring to the fore.

3 Self-marking

Having extolled the virtues of sample marking, our experience is that students often prefer to mark their own work as part of the exercise. This is because the sample might be too far removed from their own concerns. Sometimes this can be unearthed partway throughout the exercise and is most likely because (a) students want to focus on their own work, and (b) they cannot see the link between the sample and their own work.

If teachers think it best, ask students to complete a portion, draft or variant of a task, and then undertake the same activity in marking this against the rubric. There is the obvious advantage that students can apply the rubric to their own work, shedding light on what they ought to do, develop, or alter. However, it is far more difficult to control as facilitators of the exercise as students are looking at a variety of work which is unfamiliar to teachers. They may ask students to submit these for review prior to the exercise so that they can develop a plan.

Another issue may be student readiness. For example, in one unit, students were given three weeks' notice (with subsequent reminders) that they would need a rough draft of work to bring to class for this exercise. Around half of the students had prepared work; others either had not had time or did not think it important. Some did not attend the tutorial because they had nothing to bring.

4 Involvement of students in rubric development

There can be real benefits in involving students in the development of making a rubric for a task. To be clear from the outset, this approach is not for every

Devising an overall strategy for feedback 57

situation. Consider this as an activity that, in the right circumstances, is highly likely to lead to improved student work for the simple reason that they have actively been involved in decision-making about the criteria and standards to be applied to their work.

A strategy like this is suitable for advanced students, who already have a good understanding of disciplinary norms, and a developed idea about the quality of work required. However, this could also work for other students as long as they are given adequate guidance. It involves facilitating a conversation with students based on the question, "What would good work look like for this task/activity?". The rubric is then developed by all, and edited by the facilitator; students may be asked to comment on a draft before the rubric is used.

5 *Draft submission*

Depending on the size of the cohort, the nature of the task, and the level of the students, teachers/assessors may allow students to submit a draft submission so that they can receive some feedback prior to the final submission. Commonly, this could involve an outline or structure of the work they intend to submit, or a portion of it. It may be suitable for the task to be split such that a portion of the total task grade is awarded for the draft submission. This latter strategy is particularly advised for students who are new to university assessment and/or to the type of task to be completed.

6 *Peer marking*

In a self-marking exercise developed for one large unit, a peer-marking component was included. Because it was virtually impossible for the facilitator to have a conversation with each of the students about their own judgement, students were paired, and the conversation took place between them. In effect, this is a version of peer marking. With peer marking, students can swap portions of their work to be assessed against the criteria standards, and then provide verbal or written feedback to each other. (Of course, united designers will need to be mindful of the possibility of plagiarism.)

This process asks students to use the rubric to carry out a *substantive conversation*; students will need to talk to each other with a clear focus on the work and its quality. Additionally, this gives students the real feel of giving feedback, possibly developing valuable insights into the practice. One of the possible downfalls of this exercise is the facilitator's inability to control or be involved in the conversations that take place between peers. In that case, it will be beneficial to have received drafts beforehand and to have planned to sum up with key points. It is important, however, that the facilitator is able to visit each pair to listen to their conversation and provide guidance.

Within each of these exercises, make sure to discuss strategies for achieving the standards, rather than leave the discussion at what meets and what does not meet the standards. We refer to the third step stated by Sadler (1989) and

58   *Devising an overall strategy for feedback*

Hattie and Timperley (2007), wherein action is essential to *feeding forward*. We want students to have takeaway lessons from the activity which might include, for example, advice about writing and/or communication, using literature more effectively, following disciplinary conventions, etc. Feedback should also provide advice about *where* help might be sought in order to improve these skills. This might include additional resources and/or learning advisers.

7 Analysing the feedback given to the last cohort

If a teacher has taught the unit before, and assessment is similar, they can share and discuss with students a summary of the feedback given to the previous cohort. This is an extremely rich vein of resources. Of course, this means that feedback given to the last cohort of students needs to be kept, summarised and evaluated. There are several ways this can be done. One is to simply keep on hand a piece of paper or an open computer file at the time of marking on/in which to write a short statement about the feature of students' work and keep a tally of the times it has been noted. A teacher/assessor might also add notes when variations arise. Another is to use the rubrics tool within the unit's Learning Management System (LMS) that allows for downloaded summaries of marks against assessment criteria. This analysis is best combined with any of the methods above but should always include advice about action (feed forward).

Practical post-task activities: for providing feedback and feed forward

There are essentially two types of feedback as a response to student work. The first is individual feedback, and the second is general feedback. The latter is feedback given to the whole cohort of students. Within the unit design process, both individual and general feedback should be included. This feedback (how am I going?) should also include feed forward (where to next?). When the balance is right, you will see a real pay-off.

1 Individual feedback

All students deserve individual feedback on their submission, even if they are in a large cohort. Individual feedback might only be a few lines of guiding and encouraging comment, accompanied by any document mark-ups (if relevant). If students feel that they are not given *personal* feedback, they are less likely to engage with it. After all, students are interested in what *they* have done and can do better. Individual feedback thus has high value, but efficiency is something that needs to be considered with larger cohorts. Since a well-constructed rubric will provide specific feedback against marking criteria, individual feedback can be kept to a minimum by providing document mark-ups and a few summing-up sentences. For more detail on strategies for doing this well, consult Vardi (2012).

Devising an overall strategy for feedback 59

2 General feedback

This is feedback given to the whole cohort of students. The simplest way of doing this is to collect a list of common issues and strengths as you are marking, and provide this as a summary to the cohort generally, as mentioned earlier. Students can learn a lot from the work of others even if they did not personally make the specific errors. You might save several students from doing this in the future, as long as this is clear and focuses on students' future actions.

Using general feedback will reduce the time and effort needed to provide individual feedback to students. If some errors or limitations are common across the cohort, efficiencies can be found by providing general feedback once, allowing for more personalised feedback on individual students' work. Providing general feedback also helps to somewhat depersonalise negative feedback, as students realise that they have done things in common.

Giving feedback (feed up, or feed forward) is not the end of the story. Contributing to the issues we listed at the start of the chapter is the possibility or likelihood that students are not well prepared to receive and therefore *action* feedback effectively. We are all aware of students who seek their grade for a given submission, but do not read the feedback given. Similarly, we are all aware of students who read the feedback they are given, but do not adequately process it.

The following activities can be used to combat these problems, raising students' awareness of the *purpose* and *usefulness* of feedback by engaging them directly and purposefully in its examination. They are best used in class or in a synchronous online environment (as will all the activities already suggested). Even though students may value the follow-through, they may not be able to (or motivated to) follow through. That is why we recommend planning for this as part of your unit design. Schedule an activity where students learn specifically about feedback, its nature, purpose and how to use it. If the material used for the activity is the students' own feedback, they will be more engaged with the activity.

3 Pair chatting

Pair up students, each of which has chosen a point of feedback given to them. In turn, the students answer these guiding questions:

- What was the point of this feedback?
- Why did I get this feedback?
- What do I need to do next time?
- How can I make sure I do that?

The students can ask questions of, clarify misunderstandings and make suggestions to each other, thus deepening their understanding and engagement with the feedback.

60 *Devising an overall strategy for feedback*

4 Jig-saw

A teacher/assessor can choose, say, five or six of the top feedback points that were given to the students as a group. Divide the students into groups using multiples of five or six (depending on the number of points and the number of students). Each group will focus on one point only, carrying out a deep discussion about the feedback, and answering the guiding questions. Regroup the students such that one from each of the original groups is in the new groups. Have students share their discussion and its outcomes with each of the others, so that all students can engage with each of the separate feedback points. Students can make connections between the points and provide additional information/clarity.

The value of both these activities is very high, but the efficiency is perhaps best measured by the mode of instruction and the time you may allocate it in your unit schedule. These activities both put responsibility on the students to help themselves and each other to process the feedback and its implications for their work, but do so in a way that is controlled by the teacher. If each is followed by a class discussion in which key points can be drawn out, the teacher/assessor can provide clarification and guidance.

5 Individual reflections on feedback

Ask students to write a reflection in the feedback they have been given. The four simple guiding questions listed above can be used. Variations include following this by a class discussion and assigning a small portion of the grade for the next task/activity to the reflection itself. This has a high value for students, as it asks them to engage with their feedback (not just read it).

To increase the chance of students completing this task, and increasing its relevance, a small portion of the grade for the next task could be allocated to it. The questions could be posed with specific reference to the next task, for example: "What piece of feedback did you get from the last task that you have applied to this task?"; "How did you go about it?".

The quality of feedback

It can be argued, based on a model devised by Butler and Winne (1995) and informed by a wide range of research in the area, that students are central to and active in the process. Feedback comes from both external and internal sources. External sources are teachers, peers, or other supervisors. Internal feedback is generated from within as the student measures their work against the criteria and standards, and makes sense of the external feedback. Students develop knowledge, set goals, and use tactics and strategies.

Simply stating what is wrong or right about students' work after it is submitted is generally inadequate to guide them in improving their work. Formative feedback is aligned with clear criteria and standards, directed toward future learning, and

Devising an overall strategy for feedback 61

students receive guidance about *how* to improve their work in the future, not just *what* to improve.

As we have illustrated, much can be done *before* and as a task is undertaken or submitted for grading. Students can receive valuable feedback on their work or the development of their work that is likely to result in the submission of better-quality work. This reduces the need for complex or extensive feedback at marking time as a response to submitted work. An added bonus is the data so obtained, which gives the teaching academic the chance to adjust his/her teaching methods, activities and/or sequence "just-in-time".

Tunstall and Gipps (1996) distinguish between *evaluative* and *descriptive* feedback, arguing that descriptive feedback is better for students' learning. Evaluative feedback involves a value judgement – "good understanding", "excellent coverage of facts", etc., but descriptive feedback involves describing what was done and could/should be done – "minor errors in understanding...", "did not address all aspects of the task", etc. If only evaluative feedback is provided to a student, there is little provided for them to truly understand the quality of their work in the eyes of the teacher. They may know that they did well, but not know what was good about their work. At all times, the feedback needs to be closely aligned with the task and its requirements, and the rubric if there is one.

Feedback – as with feed up and feed forward – can focus on four levels: the *task*, the *processes* required, *self-regulatory* practices, and the *self/personal* (Hattie & Timperley 2007). While feedback focused at the task level is contained to how well the student achieved the specific task (for example, the degree to which it is correct or incorrect), feedback provided at the process and self-regulatory levels is more applicable to future tasks and situations. Examples of feedback provided at the self/personal level are things like "Good work" or "Great improvement". Hattie and Timperley argue that this type of feedback is the least effective for student learning but can have value insofar as building self-efficacy. Make a plan and use rubric construction to manage the focus of feedback.

One more important point: timing is of the essence. With any of these exercises, careful planning is required to optimise their positive effects. If they are planned too early, students may not be ready and/or momentum may be lost. If they are planned too late, students may not have time to be able to act on the advice they have received or developed.

Finding efficiencies

We understand that this is difficult for larger units, so consider delivering general feedback to your cohort as soon as you see patterns emerging. For example, as I am marking 100 papers I notice that a number of students are using incorrect referencing, or misunderstanding a key concept. Instead of waiting until I have marked the entire pile, which might take me another week or so, and knowing that the students will need to rectify these issues for the subsequent task, I decide

62 *Devising an overall strategy for feedback*

to post an announcement on the unit's LMS so that students can begin to incorporate that feedback into the work before their grades are released.

Summary

Feedback is inherently important in the teaching and learning process, and far more productive than simply providing a grade and a justification for a grade. Feedback is a conversation between teacher and learner, and as such should be considered as important in any teaching–learning relationship. Through feedback, students learn about their own learning, develop skills through which to judge their own work, and are motivated to make improvements.

For this to happen, however, feedback needs to have certain qualities. There is little point in providing feedback that is not understood, that is ambiguous, that does not offer advice for improvement, and/or that demoralises, antagonises or overwhelms. Such feedback is not effective for students or teachers. It is thus recommended that a feedback strategy be part of the unit design process. Thinking of what happens before and during a submission of work is just as much, if not more, important than the provision of feedback.

To develop a strategy, over the course of the teaching period create a map of the feedback that students will need and how this is going to happen. Keep in mind the seven principles of good feedback (Nicol & MacFarlane-Dick, 2006), and our key aims to address these of being formative (feeding forward), frequent, timely, relevant meaningful and actionable. Think also of workload efficiencies for markers, but mostly think about getting the best work out of the students. How can you, as a unit designer incorporate pre- and mid-task feedback exercises that yield better quality work from students? How can you incorporate exercises in engaging in feedback to reduce the gap between what you want and what students think you want? A sample unit outline, which incorporates giving feedback, is provided in Appendix F.

References

Beaumont, C., O'Doherty, M. & Shannon, L. 2011, 'Reconceptualising assessment feedback: A key to improving student learning', *Studies in Higher Education*, vol. 36, no. 6, pp. 671–687.

Butler, D.L. & Winne, P.H. 1995, 'Feedback and self-regulated learning: A theoretical synthesis', *Review of Educational Research*, vol. 65, no. 3, 245–281. https://doi.org/10.3102/00346543065003245.

Gibbs, G. 2015, '#53ideas 27 – Making feedback work involves more than giving feedback – Part 1 the assessment context' [blog post], at https://thesedablog.wordpress.com/2015/01/08/53ideas-27-part-1/.

Hattie, J. 2009, *Visible Learning: A synthesis of over 800 meta-analyses relating to achievement*, Routledge, New York.

Hattie, J. & Timperley, H. 2007, 'The power of feedback', *Review of Educational Research*, vol. 77, no. 1, pp. 81–112.

Nicol, D.J. & MacFarlane-Dick, D. 2006, 'Formative assessment and self-regulated learning: A model and seven principles of good feedback practice', *Studies in Higher Education*, vol. 31, no. 2, pp. 199–218.

Race, P. 2002, *Using Feedback to Help Students Learn*, at http://phil-race.co.uk/wp-content/uploads/Using_feedback.pdf.

Sadler, D.R. 1989, 'Formative assessment and the design of instructional systems', *Instructional Science*, vol. 18, pp. 119–144.

Tunstall, P. & Gipps, C. 1996, 'How does your teacher help you to make your work better? Children's understanding of formative assessment', *The Curriculum Journal*, vol. 7, no. 2, pp. 185–203.

Vardi, I. 2012, *Effective Feedback for Student Learning in Higher Education*, HERDSA Guide, Higher Education Research and Development Society of Australasia, Milperra, NSW.

Weaver, M.R. 2006, 'Do students value feedback? Student perceptions of tutors' written responses', *Assessment and Evaluation in Higher Education*, vol. 31, no. 3, pp. 379–394.

6 Planning effective teaching and learning experiences and activities

Introduction

Designing and developing learning experiences and activities for a unit is often referred to as *learning design* in the context of higher education. Learning design is a process that help you scaffold student learning and improve their engagement in the classroom, online or elsewhere (including in placement or internship opportunities, or during self-directed study), so that students can achieve and demonstrate the learning outcomes intended in the unit. While in Chapter 2 we emphasised the need to clearly define learning outcomes using verbs that are likely to require appropriate cognitive levels of activity, this alone is not sufficient to warrant learning.

The Intended Learning Outcomes (ILOs) become the focus for assessment, as well as teaching and learning experiences and activities. As students work toward demonstrating achievement of these ILOs, unit designers need to think about how they can build on what students bring to their learning. What should students be able to do prior to your unit? If there are key skills, how will you determine that students have the background? This will allow you to plan meaningful learning activities in order to engage and challenge students to learn and achieve *constructive alignment*.

Designing learning experiences and activities

In a "massified" higher education system, with an ever-increasing diversity of students, there is no simple answer to how we can enable students to learn in an effective, efficient, engaging and accessible way. There are also notable differences in the way students engage with learning experiences these days. With ubiquitous access to the Internet and personal devices, the boundaries between formal–informal, work–study–pleasure, personal–social and physical–virtual spaces have blurred. Students are typically enmeshed in multiple configurations of work–study–home–social commitments.

Often, students are opting to learn from off-campus locations (Bower & Kennedy 2014) and the decline in student attendance (James, Krause & Jennings 2010) is shifting the idea of a classroom and raising the question, "What learning experiences and activities are needed to structure student learning?".

The quality of teaching and learning and the associated student outcomes are key measures of success, which directly influence the quality and relevance of higher education units and courses.

To combat the issues around student participation and engagement and to reduce wasteful resources and facilities, universities have conceptualised the delivery of unit learning experiences in alternative and flexible ways. Some innovations include "flipped" classrooms, recorded lectures, "converged" delivery on multiple campus sites, and intensive delivery mode, which aim to suit the diverse needs of students. However, students are less likely to recognise value in participating if the learning activities do not directly and *explicitly* help them in completing an assessment task.

The higher education learning framework matrix developed by Carroll et al. (2018) through a synthesis of existing frameworks, literature and research, provides seven principles for making learning meaningful and the implications for teachers, students and assessment. These principles are summarised in Table 6.1.

Our aim when designing learning experiences and activities should therefore be to allow students to:

- personalise their approach to study;
- make learning decisions at the unit level;
- learn to reflect and self-evaluate their progress; and
- develop a mindset for a world of work and life-long learning.

Personalised learning can have different connotations for different students at different stages of higher education. Procedurally, this means a shift in focus from designing instruction, to designing learning interactions by considering

Table 6.1 Higher education learning framework

1	Learning as becoming	A university education provides a learning experience that broadens students' knowing and being for life beyond the classroom
2	Contextual learning	Learning occurs in context, and context can be leveraged to enhance the learning experience
3	Emotions and learning	Emotions play a role in how and why students learn
4	Interactive learning	Leverage the social dynamics of learning to enhance the learning experience
5	Learning to learn and higher-order thinking	When students employ effective methods of thinking, and understand how they learn, they can improve the way they learn
6	Learning challenge and difficulty	Challenge and difficulty can be beneficial for students' learning process
7	Deep and meaningful learning	Learning is built on connecting new understandings to prior knowledge and engages students in deep and meaningful thinking and feeling

66 *Planning teaching and learning experiences*

how the learner might respond and interact within a learning environment. It means, crucially, communicating with students that their own effort is at the centre of the learning experience.

Learning "experiences" vs learning "activities"

Generally, in higher education, learning experiences are divided into experiences that are delivered as differentiated from those that are self-directed. Delivered learning experiences are provided by teachers to their students and are not inherently classified based on the mode of delivery (that is, on a physical campus, online or blended). Delivered learning experiences encompass lectures, tutorials, seminars, workshops, studios, online activities, and the like. These learning experiences require the *active* engagement of teachers to structure, guide and unpack learning to the student. Delivered learning experiences can also include formative assessment activities as well as summative assessment activities that require the participation of the teacher for delivery. We have addressed assessment in Chapter 3.

Self-directed learning experiences, on the other hand, are those experiences that students undertake on their own. Although they may be undertaken as a result of a request from the teacher, the learning responsibility ultimately rests with the student. Self-directed learning experiences include reading, researching a topic, taking notes, summarising literature, writing reports, revising for an examination, and the like. As students move through the various year levels in their degree, and on to postgraduate study if that is the case, the complexity and quantity of self-directed learning experiences will increase. The design of learning experiences within a unit must reflect the increasing skill level of the study, as students become more competent learners progressively.

Learning activities within delivered *and* self-directed learning experiences need to be planned to improve student learning by decreasing or minimising the separation between *knowing* and *doing*. As such, learning activities can be delivered through a combination of two interdependent modes. First, learning activities can be scheduled or unscheduled. Second, the activity can be delivered synchronously (in real-time) or asynchronously (for students to complete at their own pace). The mode of student study (on a physical campus, online or blended) will determine what students are looking for and do in these pathways.

Scheduled and unscheduled activities relate to the connection that students have to their teacher and, where required, to other students studying the unit. Scheduled learning activities are an organised time such as a timetabled lecture or tutorial for physical campus students, or a designated video-chat activity for online students. They represent a commitment by both teachers and students to be present in the learning moment. Unscheduled learning activities are *ad hoc* moments such as meetings, phone calls, email, and the like, when the teacher or the student recognises a need to connect one-to-one, or many, for example, to clarify questions, or misconceptions.

Interaction between teachers/assessors and students or between students in scheduled or unscheduled learning activities can occur *synchronously* or *asynchronously*. The difference is that in synchronous learning activities, student learning is supervised directly, whereas, in asynchronous activities, student learning is supervised indirectly either before the task or after the task. This obviously relies on students' self-regulation, so explicit guidance and incentives need to be built in.

Typically, unit learning experiences are designed for synchronous collaborative learning, including rapid teacher feedback, real-time peer discussions, and an enhanced sense of connection. However, off-campus students may miss out on these experiences, as they are usually provided with asynchronous resources via Learning Management Systems (LMS) even though a synchronous learning activity may, however, be scheduled as part of an online unit offering. A challenge, therefore, is to design learning experiences that advance personalised opportunities for students irrespective of their mode of engagement with the unit.

Learning activities should be focused and linked to tasks that are framed as clear calls to action. For example, *read, watch, listen, investigate, design, solve, communicate, discuss, collaborate, integrate, evaluate, reflect*, etc. These calls for action should arise out of interactions with the teacher, with the learning and assessment resources, and with other learners (in the process of learning with and learning from each other) to enable students to achieve the ILOs.

In designing learning experiences for students, we must consider the balance between scheduled synchronous learning activities and unscheduled asynchronous learning activities to develop learner autonomy, provide opportunities for learners to develop and practise skills and tools appropriate to the discipline of study, and explore and deepen their view of the world. Good practice indicates that teachers must *initiate* the learning moment in both scheduled synchronous and unscheduled asynchronous learning activities. Formally scheduled synchronous learning activities represent delivered learning experiences, which are best suited to students in their early years of university education. Unscheduled asynchronous learning activities represent self-directed learning experiences and are typically more suited to more mature learners.

Enabling students to think and learn

University education has always been concerned with encouraging the ability to think and broadening students' thinking for life beyond the classroom. Therefore, a challenge for unit designers is to unpack the question "*What is thinking and how is it connected with the nature of academic learning?*" when designing learning activities for active student participation in delivered or self-directed learning experiences.

Cantwell (2010) explains three intersecting domains we should consider: *cognition, affect* and *metacognition*. First, students need to be able to answer questions like: What is entailed in a discipline? What does it mean to be a

68 *Planning teaching and learning experiences*

practitioner in that discipline? Why does it matter and how can I contribute to the community and society? Planning for learning involves us firstly identifying the thinking process involved with learning the concepts or skills at hand. Second, consider the likely emotional or attitudinal barriers that need to be overcome for learning to happen. How do *we* turn our students into good academic learners? What students do in their studies has the biggest impact on what students learn (Biggs & Tang 2011). Third, we need to think about how students will monitor, regulate and control their thinking and learning processes. Our methods of teaching are critical in influencing what students do and their experience.

Cognition

A simple way of defining cognition is "the use of thinking processes"; however, these processes are far from simple. We use various thinking processes depending on what we are doing. For example, if I cook dinner, I will use a variety of cognitive processes, but they would be different to the processes I will use if I drive a car. If I am cooking dinner, I might start by looking at recipe books. As I turn the pages, I am evaluating each recipe against a range of variables, posed here as questions:

- Do I have the correct ingredients (what ingredients do I have)?
- Can I replace ingredient X with ingredient Y?
- Will this take too much time (how much time do I have)?
- Do I feel like this (does this suit the current weather/season; does this appeal to my taste)? And so on...

As you can see, one particular activity can involve a significant number of low- and high-order thinking processes. Some of those processes are at a low order (for example, recalling something from memory) and others might be at a high order (for example, evaluating and creating new solutions). Low-order processes could be quick and intuitive; you may not even be aware of them. High-order processes, however, are usually more deliberate and prolonged. It is very important for teachers to understand these cognitive processes so that they can plan for, and develop, their students' learning. But this knowledge is not just useful for teachers; it is useful for learners who wish to maximise their learning potential.

Affect

Affect refers to a student's feelings about what they are thinking about. For example, when I think of a mathematics exam, I feel anxious. Why? Three very important concepts are at play here: self-concept, self-esteem and self-efficacy.

Planning teaching and learning experiences 69

Self-concept

Self-concept refers to the way we see ourselves. McInerney and McInerney (2010) define self-concept as "broadly based individual beliefs about [the] self in physical, social and academic domains" (p. 468). These beliefs can affect what we do, the way we do things, our motivations, and the like. Self-concept is formed over time. O'Mara, Marsh, Craven and Debus (2006), cited in McInerney and McInerney (2010) claim that "self-concept is formed through social interaction and social comparison" (p. 473).

As we interact with others, we gather feedback about ourselves. This feedback can be the result of how we compare ourselves to others – *I am good at mathematics, but she is better than me* – or how we compare our own individual skills – *I am good at English, so that means I am not good at mathematics.* In either case, I may well develop a negative mathematics self-concept which I could phrase as "I am not very good at maths". The same idea applies to other aspects of life.

Self-esteem

Self-esteem differs from self-concept in that it also includes an emotional response to judgement or feedback. While I might not care too much about not being good at mathematics (or being "short"), another person might rate this of high personal importance. The combination of judgement and the emotion associated with it will help determine self-worth in a particular situation, and affect the way we approach a given task (like a mathematics exam).

Self-efficacy

So, on one extreme, students may approach a task with enthusiasm, and on the other, they can approach it with great trepidation. Self-efficacy relates to a person's perceived capability of completing a task or achieving a particular outcome (McInerney & McInerney 2010). Have you ever said, "I wouldn't be able to do X" without having even tried? Why would you have said that? Could it be that you have had a bad experience in the past? Could it be that someone has expressed, implicitly or explicitly, doubt in your capabilities? Could it be a fear of "failure"? Back to that mathematics exam, a person with high self-efficacy will likely take it in their stride, whereas a person with low self-efficacy will likely face the task with fear and anxiety.

Biological impacts

There are very real biological impacts at play here. When we feel stressed, we experience the effect of adrenaline and cortisol, which are hormones that regulate, among other things, our "fight or flight" response. This can have a substantial effect on cognitive function and the function of our memory. If you are interested in reading further about this, refer to Pekrun et al. (2002) and Vogel and Schwabe (2016).

70 *Planning teaching and learning experiences*

The main effects of affect include:

- giving up versus persisting;
- surface learning versus deep learning (see section 'Enabling students to think and learn' above);
- wasting time versus making the most of time; and
- feeling confused versus feeling in control.

None of these would be new to you; we all feel them from time to time, depending on what it is we are doing or facing. External factors can have a major influence, too (for example, if someone/something else needs my attention, or the TV is turned up too loud).

This is a complex area of study. However, helping students to recognise the interplays between how they feel about themselves and others, and how they approach tasks, will be useful if we want them to take some control over their learning experiences and outcomes.

Metacognition

Metacognition involves the awareness, monitoring and control over your thinking and learning (Flavell 1979). That is, metacognition is having power over your thinking. The most successful learners regularly apply metacognitive strategies, and teachers can help to develop these through explicit and implicit teaching methods. An and Cao (2014) suggest that metacognition involves three variables: self-evaluation, understanding of the task, and available cognitive tools.

Variables are things that can change over time, and in relation with other things. We have discussed self-concept, self-esteem and self-efficacy as key ingredients for self-evaluation. But student understanding of the task at hand is crucial and in fact, can inform their self-evaluation. They could, for instance, misinterpret the task as easier, or harder, than it is. They could also completely misread the task, thinking that it is asking for something quite different. So how can we ensure that students know what they are supposed to do?

The first step is to spend time to develop an understanding of the task. Get students to read and reread the instructions, crucially and closely, and inspect the rubric provided. Unpack a task in class time, ensuring that students know what is expected and how to go about it. The second step is to help students understand the big picture, why are they being asked to do the task, how does that fit with the overall course that they are studying and what course outcomes is it aligned with? This type of insight will help them focus, and motivate them to take the first steps in learning. The third step is for students to identify the components and qualities of the task, and imagining what a good submission looks like. Much like the "visualisation" techniques that people use, this will help students to see the goal of their work.

Planning teaching and learning experiences 71

Deep and surface learning

Biggs and Tang (2011) introduce us to two students—Susan and Robert. Susan uses a "deep" approach to learning, whereas Robert uses a "surface" approach to learning. Biggs and Tang describe Susan as a student who is academically committed and switched on. She prepares for lectures, and during the lecture reflects on the significance of what she is learning. Susan wants to apply herself and do her best, and she asks questions when she doesn't understand, or when she wants to deepen her understanding. After the lecture, Susan might seek further information to satisfy her interest and desired level of understanding. She is active in her learning. Biggs and Tang describe Robert as a student who attends university simply for a qualification. He is not particularly academically committed, and just wants to pass. Robert does not prepare for lectures and attends class knowing nothing about what he will encounter. During the lecture he writes lecture notes but does not reflect on what he is learning. Later he will use these notes to recall and rote learn for the exam. He is passive in his learning.

Table 6.2, compiled by Houghton (2004), provides some valuable characteristics of approaches to learning and illustrates the importance of how unit design and planning impacts on the learning process. We obviously recommend aiming for deep learning as articulated in the table, and this means choosing and organising content-focused teaching strategies that foster it.

A focus on higher–order thinking

In order to stimulate deep learning in students it is useful for us to consider the Revised Bloom's Taxonomy (Anderson & Krathwohl 2001). We highlighted Krathwohl's (2002) two-dimensional framework in Chapter 2, in which he explains the intersection between the knowledge dimension and the cognitive process dimension ensure alignment of learning outcomes, activities and assessment tasks. The knowledge dimension classifies different types of knowledge. The cognitive process dimension represents calls for action in a continuum of increasing cognitive complexity from lower order to higher order. Table 2.3 provides the most effective way to plan learning by considering the learning activities, the learning environment, the learning outcomes and what the learners need to do to achieve the learning outcomes.

Critical thinking

Critical thinking is a process that consists of a number of subskills (i.e. analysis, evaluation and inference) that, when used appropriately, increase the chances of producing a logical solution to a problem or a valid conclusion to an argument. (Dwyer 2017, p. 77).

Table 6.2 Characteristics of deep vs surface learning

	Deep learning	*Surface learning*
Definition	• Examining new facts and ideas critically, and tying them into existing cognitive structures and making numerous links between ideas	• Accepting new facts and ideas uncritically and attempting to store them as isolated, unconnected, items
Characteristics	• Looking for meaning • Focusing on the central argument or concepts needed to solve a problem • Interacting actively • Distinguishing between argument and evidence • Making connections between different modules • Relating new and previous knowledge • Linking unit content to real life	• Relying on rote learning • Focusing on outward signs and the formulae needed to solve a problem • Receiving information passively • Failing to distinguish principles from examples • Treating parts of modules and programmes as separate • Not recognising new material as building on previous work • Seeing unit content simply as material to be learnt for the exam
Encouraged by students	• Having an intrinsic curiosity in the subject • Being determined to do well and mentally engaging when doing academic work • Having the appropriate background knowledge for a sound foundation • Having time to pursue interests, through good time management • Positive experience of education leading to confidence in ability to understand and succeed	• Studying a degree for the qualification and not being interested in the subject • Not focusing on academic areas, but emphasising others • Lacking background knowledge and understanding necessary to understand material • Not enough time/too high a workload • Cynical view of education, believing that factual recall is what is required • High anxiety

	Deep learning	*Surface learning*
Encouraged by teachers	• Showing personal interest in the subject • Bringing out the structure of the subject • Concentrating on and ensuring plenty of time for key concepts • Confronting students' perceptions • Engaging students in active learning • Using assessments that require thought, and require ideas to be used together • Relating new material to what students already know and understand • Allowing students to make mistakes without penalty, and rewarding effort • Being consistent and fair in assessing declared intended learning outcomes, and hence establishing trust	• Conveying disinterest or even a negative attitude to the material • Presenting material so that it can be perceived as a series of unrelated facts and ideas • Allowing students to be passive • Assessing for independent facts (short answer questions) • Rushing to cover too much material • Emphasising coverage at the expense of depth • Creating undue anxiety or low expectations of success by discouraging statements or excessive workload • Having a short assessment cycle

74 *Planning teaching and learning experiences*

Analysis

Recall that analysis is "the ability to identify assumptions, spot logical errors and to distinguish facts from values" (Bloom et al. 1956, cited in Booker 2007, p. 350). Dwyer further teases these out, telling us that analysis involves identifying relationships within what is presented, examining ideas to determine their role, and detecting arguments used to support claims.

Evaluation

Recall that evaluation is "the ability to judge by internal and external criteria" (Bloom et al. 1956, cited in Booker 2007, p. 350). This involves the assessment of others" statements, claims and arguments in order to determine their logical strength, their believability and to anticipate possible objections (Dwyer 2017).

Inference

This step of the process follows on to develop reasonable conclusions based on the analysis and evaluation. It involves querying evidence, conjecturing alternatives, and drawing conclusions (Dwyer 2017).

Some units contain very challenging core or fundamental concepts. Students may come to the unit with limited understanding that can contribute to misconceptions. Misconceptions can also inhibit students' learning processes and outcomes. The broader learning experience should therefore provide opportunities for these to become evident so that learning can take place in a safe and nurtured environment individually or in groups.

Using strategies such as quizzes or questioning as a means of diagnosing learning needs, can provide a learning scaffold by providing key information, evoking real-world examples and preparing students to unpack problems/scenarios through which they learn. Learning activities and resources need to be responsive. Focus the learning resources on the average student, and keep them in mind when planning learning activities. But also think about students who are below and above average. We need to respond to them too through differentiated direction in learning activities to ensure that they aren't out of their depth or bored. Learning activities should trigger a set of actions and interaction that allows students to test, practise and apply their learning.

Teaching for successful learning

Brown, Collins and Duguid (1996) argue that knowledge is situated, being in part a product of the activity, context and culture in which it is developed and used. Teaching should therefore encourage students to think about how they can situate and transfer their knowledge in the broader society in which they will live and work. Planning teaching usually begins with asking questions such as the following:

Planning teaching and learning experiences   75

1   What skills, knowledge, understanding and attitudes do students have?
2   What skills, knowledge, understanding and attitudes will be required of them in the unit?
3   What skills, knowledge, understanding and attitudes will they take away from the unit and why does it matter?
4   What support will students need in order to learn?
5   How can we include a variety of reflection and self-evaluation activities to enable perspective transformation?

Implicit in these questions are the conditional nature of knowledge, the nature of learning, the nature of motivation for learning, and the nature of social exchange of learning in a learner-centred environment that nurtures a culture of learning. In a learning culture, the focus of teaching should be on helping students become independent learners rather than on passive transfer of information to students. As experts in a discipline, teachers are well positioned to select and deliver content organised as topics or theories that can aid conceptual or philosophical transformation of students. However, this is not sufficient on its own to help students develop transferrable skills in a world where access to information is ubiquitous.

The motivation for student engagement often lies in a learner-centred environment where teachers collaborate with colleagues and students to hear what students have found to be transformational for their learning. Weimer (2002) argues that a learner-centred environment requires five key changes to practice:

1   a change in the balance of power between learner and teacher away from teacher domination towards more democratic approaches;
2   a reappraisal of the role of content away from "coverage" towards using content to develop generic skills;
3   a change in the role of teacher away from dispensing knowledge towards helping the student to learn;
4   a shift in the responsibility for managing learning away from the teacher towards the student; and
5   a change in assessment purposes and processes away from examinations towards assessment that promotes learning, including self-assessment and peer assessment.

These arguments might sound radical, but they are quite consistent with those advocated for many years by John Biggs and Paul Ramsden. In his influential text *Learning to Teach in Higher Education*, Ramsden describes teaching as follows:

> Teaching is comprehended as a process of working cooperatively with learners to help them change their understanding. It is making student learning possible. Teaching involves finding out about students'

76 *Planning teaching and learning experiences*

misunderstandings, intervening to change them and creating a context of learning that encourages students to engage with the subject matter.

(Ramsden 2003, p. 110)

Similarly, Biggs's notion of constructive alignment focuses on "what the student does", the subtitle of the book entitled *Teaching for Quality Learning at University*:

What people construct from a learning encounter depends on their motives and intentions, on what they already know, and on how they use their prior knowledge. Meaning is therefore personal. What else can it be? The alternative is that meaning is 'transmitted' from teacher to student, like dubbing an audio-tape, which is a common but untenable view.

(Biggs 2003, p. 13)

Biggs places particular emphasis on the unanticipated effects of assessment in determining how students go about learning in and out of class. The implications of the change in practice, proposed by Weimer, Ramsden and Biggs, have profound effects on how we plan our teaching. The process of planning teaching for successful learning is to clearly and explicitly articulate to you *and* to students how students will be guided for learning in the unit to achieve the *intended learning outcomes* for both in-class activities and out-of-class activities.

As we have argued earlier, we should focus on more than simply making a list of content to be covered by the unit and organising it in a particular order, even though this will likely be an outcome of the process of organising weekly or modular learning experiences within a unit. Our practice should be more than simply articulating exercises or activities to be undertaken by the students. We need to explore with students how studying the unit influences their beliefs, perceptions, social interactions and behaviours, inside and outside of the classroom.

We should also be a facilitator of knowledge, rather than being an absolute source of knowledge, and leave room for adapting learning experiences and activities based on the needs of the learning moment. This means moving away from an inclination to simply state "*complete exercises on …*", or to write "*discuss …*" but, we should think about the success criteria: *what is the result of the completed exercises or the engagement in discussion and why does it matter?* This way, the outcomes of their engagement in learning activities are made visible, which in turn provides evidence for their learning progress.

Effectively planned learning experiences and activities should aid students to regulate and control their own thinking and learning processes (that is, aid the development of metacognitive strategies). Teaching activities can then bring to the fore and unpack the likely conceptual, emotional or attitudinal barriers that need to be overcome for learning to happen. The following questions in Table 6.3, adapted from the *Teaching for Effective Learning Framework* (Department of Education 2015) form a useful tool to document learning design and prepare for how we can build on students' prior knowledge, skills and understanding and challenge them in their thinking and learning.

Planning teaching and learning experiences 77

Table 6.3 Documenting learning design

What do we want them to learn?	What is the intended learning? Why does it matter?	What do they bring?
So, how will we know if they have learnt it?	What will the intended learning look like at this level? What is the minimum standard?	What will signal student progress and success towards the minimum standard?
Now, what will we do to get there?	How will we engage, challenge and support their learning?	What will be the plan for each week or module of learning?

Characteristics of effective learning experiences and activities

When developing unit learning activities, we often tend to focus on the activities and instructions, rather than the *outputs* of the instruction. This can lead to a student perception that learning is the activity, when in fact, learning is derived from careful consideration of the *meaning* of the activity. Wiggins and McTighe (1998) argue that learning activities should be derived from the learning outcomes expected of students, and not from methods, books and activities with which we are most comfortable. We agree – after all, what is the point of a teaching activity if it does not result in learning, and contribute to the overall learning experience of students? They recommend that learning activities should be designed with the following considerations:

- What should the students know and be able to do? What enduring understandings are desired?
- What will teachers accept as evidence that learning has taken place?
- What learning activities will best support students to achieve the learning outcomes?

These questions highlight their framework called *backwards mapping* (Chapter 2), which naturally encourages unit designers to establish the purpose of doing something before implementing it into the unit curriculum. The incorporation of backward mapping also lends itself to transparent and explicit teaching, which occurs in three stages guided by the three questions above. The first stage is about identifying the desired results, the second stage is about determining acceptable evidence of learning, and the third stage is about planning learning experiences and instructions.

If you have defined the outcomes for each of the learning activities in the unit, then you are likely to have a better idea of what you want students to get out of each learning activity. This way, you can have a clear vision of a variety of low-stakes (simpler) and high-stakes (more complex) learning activities that would work best to activate student learning and leverage the experience and outcomes that you want them to achieve.

78 *Planning teaching and learning experiences*

Active learning is a key feature of well-planned learning activities. *Active learning* is designed as "students doing things and thinking about what they are doing" (Bonwell & Eison 1991). The aim of active learning is to provide opportunities for learners to not just think about what they are doing, but also about why they are doing that in learning activities to deepen and challenge their understanding. A range of low-stakes and high-stakes learning activities are listed in Table 6.4 along with their features, the experiences that they can stimulate, the cognitive outcomes that you can help students develop, and the potential of that activity for encouraging deep learning.

Summary

If designed, sequenced and documented well, the learning experiences planned for a unit can be a useful guide to students for undertaking study, as much as it can be a useful guide for the teaching team to help students to learn. Here are some suggestions for designing learning experiences:

- Practically, organising the learning experience of the unit is best done with input from others (if this is available). Your colleagues or educational designers may see alternative structures, and provide you with constructive feedback.
- If you are redesigning a unit, consider any difficulties students may have had in the previous offering, as well as the strengths of the previous structure/organisation.
- Aim to maximise "in-class" or synchronous online time by programming appropriate learning activities as "out-of-class" or asynchronous online activities. What needs your immediate supervision, and what does not? This may well depend on the level of your students. You might like to read up on the "flipped classroom", or Just in Time Teaching (JiTT) (Novak 2011) for ideas and principles.
- Find themes within your unit's content, and consider modularising the unit. For example, an enabling education unit was arranged around three themes: learning about learning, learning about students, and learning about teaching. In order, these three built up the students' understanding of education. Assessments were structured to develop these understandings (learning about learning was aimed at students' own learning), and finally, students were asked to "put it all together" through applying their understanding to a number of scenarios in the final assessment. Of course, this structure may not suit your unit, but it shows one way of organising the learning experience of the unit such that it strategically builds from simple to complex, from (relatively) easy to difficult both within modules and overall.
- Particularly (but not exclusively) for enabling and first-year students, your focus will be on developing certain academic literacies/skills, whether they are general or discipline-specific. Do not overlook these when planning the overall learning experience of the unit. Consider what is required of

Table 6.4 Characteristics of learning activities

Activity	Features	Experience	Engagement	Cognitive outcome	Potential for promoting deep learning
Direct instruction	Lectures, demonstrations, explanation without a great deal of student input	Demonstrating a skill or procedure; introducing knowledge	On campus; online (synchronous or asynchronous)	Remember – understand	Low
Quiz	Students demonstrate skills/ knowledge in a short-form test	Application of skills and knowledge	On campus; online (synchronous or asynchronous)	Remember – apply	Low
Reading	Students find or are given relevant article/s to read and comprehend	Extending student under-standing; providing a foundation for further learning	On campus; online (synchronous or asynchronous)	Remember – evaluate	Low–High
Watching a video	Students find or are given relevant videos to watch and comprehend	Extending student under-standing; providing a foundation for further learning	On campus; online (synchronous or asynchronous)	Remember – evaluate	Low–High
Guided discussion	Students engage in mean-ingful conversation with each other, guided by cri-tical questions	Eliciting varying ideas; providing a forum for student input; in-depth exploration of an idea; forming and articulating thoughts	On campus; online (synchronous or asynchronous)	Remember – evaluate	High
Problem solving	Students engage in solving a problem, ethical dilemma	Eliciting varying approa-ches and processes; devel-oping problem-solving methodologies; developing critical reasoning skills; testing hypotheses	On campus; online (synchronous or asynchronous)	Apply – create	High

(Continued)

Table 6.4 (Cont.)

Activity	Features	Experience	Engagement	Cognitive outcome	Potential for promoting deep learning
Small- group/ team work	Three or more students working together with or without direct intervention of a teacher	Providing a forum for student input; developing collaborative and communication skills	On campus; online (synchronous)	Remember – create	High
Role play	Dramatisation of a situation, concept or point of view	Exploring different points of view; applying current knowledge and skills; developing collaborative and communication skills; challenging and broadening personal conceptions of real world	On campus; online (synchronous or asynchronous)	Apply – create	High
Case study	Exploration of a real-life narrative	Exploring different points of view; applying current knowledge and skills; developing questioning and reasoning skills; encouraging critical thinking and problem-solving skills	On campus; online (synchronous or asynchronous)	Apply – evaluate	High
Debate	Examines opposing points of view on a given topic (response to a given statement)	Exploring different points of view; applying current knowledge and skills; developing questioning and reasoning skills; encouraging critical thinking and problem-solving skills	On campus; online (synchronous or asynchronous)	Remember – create	High

Planning teaching and learning experiences   81

students to understand content and/or perform particular tasks and build these in at strategic points. For example, it may not be wise to engage students in an activity such as a debate early in the unit, when they may not have developed conceptual or communicative skills to do so successfully. This learning activity could backfire, leaving you with more work to do in terms of clearing-up issues. The same applies to any assessment tasks. We recommend a "just-in-time" approach where students are taught academic literacies/skills at strategically important points throughout the unit such that they can be immediately applied and formatively assessed. The *Student Success Journal*, formerly known as *The International Journal of the First Year in Higher Education*, is a good source of information about this.

- Learning design in your unit will also be optimised if you are able to align it with content, skills and knowledge that your students may be learning in other units. We recognise that this is often rather tricky territory, especially if your unit is an elective or a service unit. However, as mentioned previously, good principles of overall course design should take into account the relationships between individual units such that student learning is made more connected and thus meaningful.

References

An, Y.-J. & Cao, L. 2014, 'Examining the effects of metacognitive scaffolding on students' design problem solving in an online environment', *MERLOT Journal of Online Learning and Teaching*, vol. 10, no. 4, pp. 552–568.

Anderson, L. & Krathwohl, D. 2001, *A Taxonomy for Learning, Teaching and Assessing: A revision of Bloom's taxonomy of educational objectives*, Longman, New York.

Biggs, J.B. 2003, *Teaching for Quality Learning at University: What the student does*, 2nd edn, The Society for Research into Higher Education (SRHE) and Open University Press, Maidenhead, Berkshire.

Biggs, J.B., & Tang, C.S.-K. 2011. *Teaching for Quality Learning at University: What the student does*, 4th edn, The Society for Research into Higher Education (SRHE) and Open University Press, Maidenhead, Berkshire.

Bloom, B.S. (ed.), Engelhart, M.D., Furst, E.J., Hill, W.H., & Krathwohl, D.R. 1956, *Taxonomy of educational objectives: The classification of educational goals. Handbook 1: Cognitive domain*, David McKay, New York.

Bonwell, C. & Eison, J. 1991, *Active Learning: Creating excitement in the classroom*, ERIC Clearing House and Association for the Study of Higher Education, Washington, DC.

Booker, M.J. 2007, 'A roof without walls: Benjamin Bloom's Taxonomy and the misdirection of American education', *Academic Questions*, vol. 20, no. 4, pp. 347–355.

Bower, M. & Kennedy, J. 2014, *Blended Synchronous Learning*, Macquarie University and the Australian Government Office for Learning and Teaching, Sydney.

Brown, J.S., Collins, A. & Duguid, P. 1996, 'Situated cognition and the culture of learning', in H. McLellan (ed.), *Situated Learning Perspectives*, Educational Technology Publications, Englewood Cliffs, NJ, pp. 19–44.

Butler, D.L. & Winne, P.H. 1995, 'Feedback and self-regulated learning: A theoretical synthesis', *Review of Educational Research*, vol. 65, no. 3, 245–281. https://doi.org/10.3102/00346543065003245.

82 *Planning teaching and learning experiences*

Cantwell, R. 2010, 'The nature of academic learning', in R. Cantwell & J. Scevak (eds), *An Academic Life*, ACER Press, Melbourne, Australia.

Carroll, A., Lodge, J., Bagraith, R., Nugent, A., Matthews, K. & Sah, P. 2018, *Higher Education Learning Framework: An evidence informed model for university learning*, The University of Queensland, Brisbane, Australia.

Department of Education, SA 2015, *Using TfEL for Learning Design*, The Government of South Australia, at https://acleadersresource.sa.edu.au/resources/teaching-for-effective-learning-resources/using-tfel-for-learning-design.

Dwyer, C.P. 2017, *Critical Thinking: Conceptual perspectives and practical guidelines*, Cambridge University Press, Cambridge.

Flavell, J.H. 1979, 'Metacognition and cognitive monitoring: A new area of cognitive–developmental inquiry', *American Psychologist*, vol. 34, no. 10, pp. 906–911.

Houghton, W. 2004, *Learning and Teaching Theory for Engineering Academics*, The Higher Education Academy Engineering Subject Centre, York.

James, R., Krause, K.-L. & Jennings, C. 2010, *The First Year Experience in Australian Universities: Findings from 1994 to 2009*, The University of Melbourne, Melbourne, Australia.

Krathwohl, D. 2002, 'A revision of Bloom's Taxonomy: An overview', *Theory into Practice*, vol. 41, no. 4, pp. 212–218.

McInerney, D. & McInerney, V. 2010, *Educational Psychology: Constructing learning*, 5th edn, Frenchs Forest NSW and Pearson Australia, NSW, Australia.

Novak, G.M. 2011, 'Just-in-time teaching', *New Directions for Teaching and Learning*, vol. 2011, no. 128, pp. 63–73.

O'Mara, A.J., Marsh, H.W., Craven, R.G. & Debus, R.L. 2006, 'Do self-concept interventions make a difference? A synergistic blend of construct validation and meta-analysis', *Educational Psychologist*, vol. 41, no. 3, pp. 181–206.

Pekrun, R., Goetz, T., Titz, W. & Perry, R.P. 2002, 'Academic emotions in students' self-regulated learning and achievement: A program of qualitative and quantitative research', *Educational Psychologist*, vol. 37, no. 2, pp. 91–106.

Ramsden, P. 2003, *Learning to Teach in Higher Education*, 2nd edn, RoutledgeFalmer, New York.

Vogel, S. & Schwabe, L. 2016, 'Learning and memory under stress: implications for the classroom', *npj Science of Learning*, vol. 1, art. 16011.

Weimer, M. 2002, *Learner Centred Teaching: Five key changes to practice*, 1st edn, Jossey-Bass, San Francisco, CA.

Wiggins, G. & McTighe, J. 1998, *Understanding by Design*, Jossey-Bass, San Francisco, CA.

7 Evaluating the design of your unit

Introduction

In Chapters 1 and 2, we highlighted the importance of *curriculum alignment* through *coherent course and unit design*. Here, we turn to planning for unit design evaluation. It is important to note that we are not focused on *unit performance* as such, which is usually measured in terms of student feedback, grade breakdowns, academic integrity referrals or student complaints (if there are any). Rather, we are interested in the *quality* of the unit design and ways to measure that quality.

By now, as a unit designer, you will have made many decisions about unit ILOs and experiences, assessments, rubrics, and feedback ... Were they good ones? Could they be better? This chapter is about giving you some strategies and tools for planning systematic evaluation and continuous improvements to curriculum, learning and teaching, and assessment plans, and practice. The type and frequency of evaluation will differ from unit to unit, from teacher to teacher, and from one institution to another. Differences may be due to mode of unit delivery, the teaching academic's personal goals, institutional policies and procedures among other things. Whichever way evaluation is carried out – be it one-off, iterative, immediate or longitudinal – it involves reflective practice.

Conducting systematic review to improve unit quality

The primary purpose of conducting and documenting systematic unit design evaluation is to ensure that the design of a unit is of high quality and that it contributes to improvements in student learning. From a quality assurance perspective, in the Australian context, the quality of a unit is evaluated through a comprehensive review of "the design and content, expected learning outcomes, the methods for assessment of those outcomes, the extent of students' achievement of learning outcomes, and also takes account of emerging developments in the field of education, modes of delivery, the changing needs of students and identified risks to the quality of the course of study" (Birmingham 2015). We have expanded this in Table 7.1 to illustrate what is essential for undertaking a review and the questions that unit designers should tackle.

84   *Evaluating the design of your unit*

Table 7.1 Unit design evaluation criteria

No.	Criteria	Questions
1	Strategic rationale	Does the strategic rationale explain the context that underpins the design of this unit?
2	Intended learning outcomes	Do the ILOs clearly explain what students will be able to do upon completion of the unit?
3	The methods for assessment of those outcomes	Will the unit assessment strategy drive learning?
4	The extent of students' achievement of learning outcomes	How will the teaching team differentiate between satisfactory achievement of ILOs and exceptional achievement of ILOs?
5	Takes account of emerging developments in the field of education	How is emerging new knowledge incorporated into unit content?
6	Content of the unit	What academic and industry benchmarking has been undertaken to ensure that the content of the unit is contemporary?
7	Modes of delivery	How does the teaching team use delivery modes to improve inclusiveness and how comparable is the learning experience across different delivery modes?
8	The changing needs of students	How does the unit design plan to capitalise on the diversity of the students?
9	Identified risks to the quality of the unit	What does the review team see as the major risks to unit quality and how are these mitigated?

Reflective practice

From a scholarly teaching perspective, review of unit quality will involve reflection for action rather than review. John Dewey (1933) reasoned that an individual usually reflects when there is real problem or a sense of difficulty by merely "thinking" about them. He recommended three steps of reflection: (1) problem definition; (2) analysis; and (3) generalisation. Through his analysis on reflection, he explained the difference between taking action based on thinking and reasoning, as opposed to impulsive reaction. Reflective practice involves a *deliberate, systematic* and *critical analysis* of one's work with an aim to improving it.

Research into good teaching practice that followed highlighted the purpose of reflection as a tool for addressing the ultimate aim, which is improving student learning. Brookfield (1998) identified "Four Lenses" for investigating the question that many good teachers have: "How do I know if what I am doing is working and making a difference to student learning?" The four lenses that he suggests using are: (1) students' perspective; (2) peers' feedback; (3) your own experiences as a learner and a teacher; and (4) scholarly literature on teaching and learning to gather evaluative data. Receiving the support and endorsement of academic colleagues, teaching and learning experts and in fact students who will be most affected by the design of a unit is key for the success of a unit.

So, the problem that we have identified for unit designers is: *How will you convince yourself, your colleagues and your students that your design will improve student learning?* This needs unit designers to think about:

- who the stakeholders are;
- what their motivations and priorities could be;
- what evidence will you gather to convince for their investment in terms of time and resources;
- how will you convince students about your assumptions and expectations; etc.

Essentially, we want unit designers to reflect on the design, and prepare counterfactual statements, reasons and justifications with evidence that will help them arrive to the conclusion that their design can improve student learning. This is where Brookfield's Four Lenses becomes useful. We recognise, however, that gathering evidence from students can be tricky before the unit is delivered.

Students' perspectives

The idea of students as partners can create a space for unit designers to work together with students in testing assumptions and decisions, but it is still a dilemma for higher education as the role of student partners is not a well-defined or well-evidenced area for shaping curriculum, learning and teaching, and assessment practice. Although we suggest caution, we cannot think of any reason why we should not be involving students as partners to test the design of a unit before its implementation and shape their learning experience.

The idea of students as partners for testing and validating unit design is very similar to testing any product design for reliability before large-scale production. As we highlighted in the previous chapter, in a learning culture the focus of teaching should be on helping students become independent learners, in which the student–teacher relationship is at the heart of teaching and learning dialogue.

Dunne and Zandstra (2011) argue that there is value in pushing students out of their comfort zone, challenging the logic of their thinking and enabling them as change agents to take responsibility for their learning. They highlight a subtle, but extremely important difference between universities that "listen" to student feedback through surveys and "respond accordingly" and universities that provide students "the opportunity" to explore areas that they believe to be significant, actively participate as collaborators and co-producers and recommend solutions and changes that are required.

Of course, students need to be carefully selected and inducted into unit design evaluation process. Induction should focus on developing their understanding of the scope of their involvement and outcomes expected, but

86 *Evaluating the design of your unit*

students can be the best source of evaluative data for any unit designer. Unit designers should remember to ask students to respond to the planned unit intent, learning outcomes, learning activities and experiences, assessments and rubrics, and to feedback that is planned for the unit.

Essentially, ask them to think about what they want to do well in this unit. Find out about what that means to them. Do they think that the assessment tasks are too hard, or too easy? Do they see any connections between the scheduled learning activities and the assessment tasks? Do they think that the mix of individual and group activities is appropriate? Unit designers should reflect on students' reactions to their explanation of the unit design and see if they have been able to match student expectations.

Healey, Flint and Harrington (2014) made an impassioned plea that the partnership values presented in Table 7.2 are extremely important to acknowledge and practice and to ensure that the relationship unit designers have with students is a productive one.

Once the unit is delivered, unit designers, along with teachers and assessors, can compare their reflection of student responses to unit design with the observations, analysis and reflections they make during the delivery of the unit. The sources of data can be previous student feedback (if not the first time of delivery of the unit), notes about student engagement in learning activities and

Table 7.2 Students as partners: partnership values and definition

No.	Partnership values	Definition
1	Authenticity	The rationale for all parties to invest in partnership is meaningful and credible
2	Honesty	All parties are honest about what they can contribute to partnership and about where the boundaries of partnership lie
3	Inclusivity	There is equality of opportunity and any barriers (structural or cultural) that prevent engagement are challenged
4	Reciprocity	All parties have an interest in, and stand to benefit from, working and/or learning in partnership
5	Empowerment	Power is distributed appropriately and ways of working and learning promote healthy power dynamics
6	Trust	All parties take time to get to know one-another and can be confident they will be treated with respect and fairness
7	Courage	All parties are encouraged to critique and challenge practices, structures and approaches that undermine partnership, and are enabled to take risks to develop new ways of working and learning
8	Plurality	All parties recognise and value the unique talents, perspectives and experiences that individuals contribute to partnership
9	Responsibility	All parties share collective responsibility for the aims of the partnership, and individual responsibility for the contribution that they make

Evaluating the design of your unit 87

informal assessment of their understanding, the quality of student assessment submissions, feedback provided to students on their work in general, student questions asked via discussion forum, email or in class, and other strategic questionnaires, focus groups or interviews, and unsolicited feedback.

Here are some guiding questions:

- Were students engaged and interactive?
- What was the quality of their work?
- What were the main issues they had?
- What questions were most asked?
- What feedback did you have to give them?
- What did you learn about your assumptions about them?

When unit designers do plan to get feedback from students via strategic questionnaires, focus groups or interviews, they should focus the questions and frame them well so that the evaluation is accurate and useful. They should also time the evaluation well: if time has passed between an event and the time they asked students for their evaluation (for example, a lecture), they may be likely to provide an evaluation that is not reliable. For more on gaining student feedback, we recommend Davis (2009), who outlines a number of different approaches which can be implemented at suitable times throughout a unit.

Peer feedback

Planning for peer-evaluation should not happen as an afterthought. It is wise for any unit designer, teacher and/or assessor to strategically plan peer-evaluation at different stages throughout the unit design process, and document that evaluation so that they are not trying to remember what happened at these stages. This book is situated on the premise that unit designers will engage with peer feedback through the act of designing a unit. The first step is to analyse the *context* for design. Analysing the context requires unit designers to develop a strategic rationale for the unit, considering the bigger purpose, the place of the unit within a degree course and its importance for student learning within and beyond the course.

In Chapter 1, we provided a rationale for developing the strategic rationale for a unit will require unit designers to identify the individuals that they will talk with, to get their perspectives for defining the scope for the unit. These individuals could be the unit caretakers for the unit that is preceding or succeeding the unit that they are designing or redesigning within a course, or they have a greater role in reviewing the quality of and governing academic programmes. These individuals are people unit designers may need to go back to several times during the evaluation stages that they have planned for the unit. The partnership values that we highlighted in Table 6.1 are equally important to uphold with peers as well to check if the unit design goals match the outcomes that have been achieved and how that gels with their thinking.

88 *Evaluating the design of your unit*

Unit designers will do well to document their reflection of their reactions and perspectives. These will come in handy when there is a conflict of interest or if they need to revisit a critical decision that was made during the design process, be it ILOs, key summative assessment tasks, feedback strategies or others that might need resource allocation for unit delivery.

Teaching peers are also extremely valuable as a source of evaluative data. We recommend that unit designers ask a trusted colleague within the unit teaching team, or otherwise, to provide constructive comments on specific aspects of the unit design. This may include asking for their feedback on the alignment: of assessment tasks with unit outcomes; of teaching and learning activities with assessment tasks; of feedback to a given rubric or set of criteria. Additionally, unit designers could schedule a classroom visit during which they could look specifically at student learning experiences, especially if they have planned on implementing a learning activity that is new to them or the unit. There are many models or frameworks associated with peer review of teaching, but they all have something more or less in common, and that is the process:

- Set goals (define what is to be reviewed and why).
- Develop strategies (figure out how to go about the review).
- Carry out the evaluation.
- Make decisions based on the evaluation.
- Put them into practice.

With peer review, unit designers can opt for a mentor–mentee relationship (for example, consulting with someone they know well and who has particular expertise in an area in which they would like to improve), a peer–peer relationship (working with one another in a reciprocal fashion), or a strategic relationship (working with someone in order to develop closer connections). For detailed information about peer observation, consult Bell (2012).

Self-evaluation

Self-evaluation is the process of checking for oneself if one has been able to achieve one's stated goals. It can be an effective tool to self-regulate one's ability to design units effectively for higher education courses. Without thinking about where they stand and how they are doing with respect to their own goals for unit design, it is plainly impossible for a unit designer to provide feedback for unit design. Taylor, Neter and Wayment (1995) argue that the motivations for self-evaluation can be varied. In characterising the literature on self-evaluation, they recommend that the process of self-evaluation should include self-assessment, self-enhancement, self-verification and self-improvement to not only feel better about oneself, but to demonstrate the capacity to get better at doing something.

In the case of unit design, the motive for the unit designer is to *get better at designing units*. Self-evaluation should therefore focus on identifying one's own

Evaluating the design of your unit 89

limitation to design and consequently set goals for improvement. Throughout the book, we have provided questions and examples to guide unit designers' self-evaluation in the process of designing a unit. We recommend that they generate a response first based on their experience as a learner, or a teacher or both, before seeking input or feedback for their response. When unit designers consult with peers or student partners to check their response, they should ascertain whether those commentators' thinking matches theirs. Unit designers should ask themselves if there are any fundamental differences in the commentators' thinking with that of their own, for example, are there any philosophical differences, or any pedagogical differences? They should then consider if there will be the impact or consequence of their opinion on their design decisions.

Brookfield (2006) suggests that self-evaluation involves putting our autobiographical selves in the mirror to understand students' experiences through self-reflection. Reflection happens when one draws on one's own experiences as a learner and one's understanding about how students (adults) learn. Reflection alerts us to assumptions that we have made along the way. Testing our assumptions with peers and students and reflecting on their responses allows us to plan for self-improvement. Kolb (2014) describes this process as *experiential learning* or learning from experiences. In the first phase of his experiential learning model, the learner has a specific experience of learning, in the second the learner observes and reflects on the experience of learning, in the third observations are related to other concepts in the learner's past experience and knowledge and in the last phase the learner develops capacity to identify implications of action that can be tested and applied to other situations.

Self-evaluation, leading to self-improvement for designing units follows a similar model, where in the first phase the designer brings their own "concrete" experience of designing units or at least learning experiences as adult learners. In the second phase, using the chapters in this book as stages, the designer notices their design and reflects through self-evaluation, and then by checking with peers and student partners. In the third stage the designer assesses the designed outcomes against their goals, and relates the unit design approach that we have provided with other models for unit design or their own past experience and knowledge. By reflecting on their outcomes, the designer prepares reasoned arguments to *convince themselves, their colleagues and their students that their design will improve student learning.*

Another self-reflection model offered by Driscoll (2000) is to think about the whole event using three simple questions: "What?"; "So what?"; and "Now what?". These three questions are also useful to aid unit designers to think about, for example, *what* are the unit ILOs, *so what* learning and assessment activities will enable students to develop evidence for achieving those ILOs, *now what* should the teacher do to help them achieve that. Thinking about and reflecting on "what" enables the designer to return to the situation, "so what" enables a deeper understanding of the context, "now what" helps them modify future outcomes.

90   *Evaluating the design of your unit*

Summary

While we have provided some recommendations around who could be used to source evaluation data, it is important to devise an evaluation plan using sound evaluation practice. Documenting the review allows for closing the loop, as needed, particularly to students so that they know that you have taken their feedback on board. We have provided a worksheet in Appendix G to complete at the point of unit design, and keep handy throughout unit delivery as a timetable and/or log to document thinking and reflection. The following checklist adapted from Caffarella (2002) can also be useful in designing a systematic unit design evaluation:

- Have you secured support for the evaluation from those who have a stake in the results of the evaluation?
- Have you identified the individuals who plan and oversee the evaluation?
- Have you defined precisely the purpose of evaluation and how the results are to be used?
- Have you specified what is to be judged and formulated the evaluation questions?
- Have you determined who supplies the needed evidence and if some of that data are already available?
- Have you delineated the evaluation approach chosen the data collection techniques to be used, when the data are to be collected, and/or how the existing data can be put into useable forms?
- Have you indicated the method of data analysis and stipulated the criteria to use when making judgements about the unit or established the process to be applied in determining the criteria?
- Have you determined the specific timeline, and the resources needed for evaluation?
- Have you planned how to monitor and complete the evaluation and make judgements about the ways in which the evaluation data can be used to improve the design?

References

Bell, M. 2012, *Peer Observation Partnerships in Higher Education*, 2nd edn, Higher Education Research and Development Society of Australasia, Milperra, NSW.

Birmingham, S. 2015, *Higher Education Standards Framework (Threshold Standards) 2015*, Department of Education and Training, Australian Government, Federal Register of Legislative Instruments.

Brookfield, S. 1998, 'Critically reflective practice', *Journal of Continuing Education in the Health Professions*, vol. 18, no. 4, pp. 197–205.

Brookfield, S.D. 2006, *The Skillful Teacher: On technique, trust, and responsiveness in the classroom*, 2nd edn, Jossey-Bass, San Francisco, CA.

Caffarella, R.S. 2002, *Planning Programs for Adult Learners: A practical guide for educators, trainers and staff developers*, 2nd edn, vol. 1, Jossey-Bass, New York.

Davis, B.G. 2009, *Tools for Teaching*, 2nd edn, Jossey-Bass, San Francisco, CA.

Dewey, J. 1933, *How We Think: A restatement of the relation of reflective thinking to the educative process*, D.C. Heath, Boston, MA.

Driscoll, J. 2000, *Practising Clinical Supervision*, Bailièrre Tindall, Edinburgh.

Dunne, E. & Zandstra, R. 2011, *Students as Change Agents: New ways of engaging with learning and teaching in Higher Education*, ESCalate, Bristol.

Healey, M., Flint, A. & Harrington, K. 2014, *Engagement Through Partnership: Students as partners in learning and teaching in higher education*, Higher Education Academy, York.

Kolb, D. 2014, *Experiential Learning: Experience as the source of learning and development*, 2nd edn, Pearson Education, Upper Saddle River, NJ.

Taylor, S., Neter, E. & Wayment, H. 1995, 'Self-evaluation processes', *Society for Personality and Social Psychology*, vol. 21, no. 12, pp. 1278–1287.

Appendices

Appendix A. Initial unit analysis (Chapter 1)

Table A1: Initial analysis: An evaluation sheet to analyse the context for unit design

Unit characteristics	Questions for consideration	Pointers	Your notes
Purpose	<ul><li>What is the purpose of this unit?</li><li>What is the year level of the unit?</li><li>What course(s) does the unit sit within and why?</li><li>What are the prerequisites for study in this unit and what other units have this unit as a prerequisite?</li><li>What learning expectations are placed on this unit by the discipline, course or professional accreditation bodies?</li></ul>	<ul><li>Explain the need for this unit from a student perspective</li><li>Explain the need from a discipline perspective</li><li>Explain the need for this unit from a value-added perspective</li></ul>	
Aims	<ul><li>What does the unit aim for students to develop, progress and apply?</li><li>What is the key knowledge?</li><li>What are the key skills?</li><li>What is the main learning intended?</li></ul>	<ul><li>Explain the nature of learning from a student perspective. Is learning sequential, or otherwise</li><li>Explain the most significant concepts and skills that students must achieve</li></ul>	
Learning outcomes	<ul><li>What are the intended learning outcomes?</li><li>How are students reminded of the intended learning outcomes throughout the unit?</li><li>How are the unit components linked to the intended learning outcomes?</li></ul>	<ul><li>Evaluate and explain alignment of unit components including assessment tasks, course-level learning outcomes and graduate learning outcomes</li></ul>	
Assessment tasks	<ul><li>What is the purpose of assessment in this unit?</li><li>How are the assessment tasks aligned with the unit learning outcomes?</li><li>What course level and graduate learning outcomes are assessed in this unit?</li><li>What must every student know, do and demonstrate in order to complete the assessment tasks successfully?</li><li>How can they demonstrate evidence of learning outcomes they attained?</li><li>What are the assessment tasks?</li><li>Are there any formal yet authentic (real-world or applied) assessment tasks?</li></ul>	<ul><li>Explain the purpose of assessment from a student learning perspective</li><li>Explain acceptable standards of student performance</li><li>Evaluate the alignment of assessment and the suitability of assessment methods in the unit to elicit intended learning outcomes</li><li>Clarify the nature of student work and the format that they should use when submitting assessment work samples</li></ul>	

Appendices   93

Unit characteristics	Questions for consideration	Pointers	Your notes
Learning experiences	• What knowledge and skills are assumed? • What is the nature of the content? • How are learning experiences delivered in the unit? • What study contact is expected? (Individual work, group work, workplace learning) • What is the length and frequency of classes, practicums, online seminars, etc? • What does the learning environment look like? • What infrastructure resources and space are required?	• Explain what experiences can students expect in the unit? (on campus, online or both) • Explain how students enrolled in multiple mode of unit delivery will engage in the learning opportunities? • Explain if content is theoretical, practical or a combination, and what preparation is expected of students before hand? What follow-up is needed after their engagement with learning activities?	
Student characteristics	• How many students are expected to enrol in the unit? • What does the student enrolment pattern look like in the unit? • What are any known student needs for study in this unit? • How will students be supported if they have specific needs for engagement in the unit?	• Explore student characteristics and document considerations for unit design and delivery	
Your characteristics	• What beliefs and values do you have about teaching and learning? • What is your philosophy towards assessment? • How will you support, motivate and encourage student learning in this unit? • What professional development would you need to effectively design and deliver this unit?	• Think about your needs and your experiences • Identify your approaches to teaching and learning and evaluate if your approaches match the unit design and delivery requirements • Request professional development as needed	

Appendix B. **Checking ILOs (Chapter 2)**

Table B1: ILO Checker: An evaluation sheet for unit designers

Outcome	Student centred?	Demonstrable?	Measurable?	Achievable?	Clear?	Meaningful?	Relevant?
At the end of this unit, students will be able to …	Is the ILO focused on what the students will be able to do at the end of the unit?	Are you able to witness evidence of achievement of this ILO?	Are you able to measure how well students are doing this? Are you able to grade this?	Who are your students? Are they capable of achieving this outcome?	Is the ILO clear about what students will be able to do?	Is the ILO meaningful, or is it trivial?	Is the ILO able to be clearly mapped to course / discipline outcomes?
1							
2							
3							
4							
5							
6							

Relevant – If the outcome does not go some way towards meeting those at a higher level (e.g. course-level and discipline-level outcomes), it is not relevant.

Appendices 95

Appendix C. ILO planning (Chapter 2)

At the end of this unit, student should be able to ...
Or
On successful completion of this unit, students will be able to ...

Table C1: ILO planning sheet

1	
2	
3	
4	
5	
6	

Remember that good learning outcomes are:

Student Centred: Learning outcomes express what the *students* will be able to do at the end of a learning session/unit/course.

Demonstrable: students will have an opportunity to show you that they have achieved this outcome, by doing something. Careful use of verbs is important.

Measurable: You need to be able to measure the quality of the students' work in able to assess their learning against the outcome. How do you measure appreciation?

Achievable: It needs to be reasonable that students can achieve the outcome in the given time-frame and context. You may need to revise and/or qualify the level of achievement.

Clear: Being overly ambiguous does not provide clarity for the teacher or student. Try to be clear without being overly specific.

Meaningful: Some outcomes are trivial in context, and may go without saying. Get rid of these, or amend another to address them.

Relevant: If the outcome does not go some way towards meeting those at a higher level (e.g. course-level and discipline-level), it is not relevant.

96 *Appendices*

Appendix D. Evaluating assessment (Chapter 3)

Table D1: Worksheet for evaluating the suitability of assessment tasks

Task	Alignment	Suitability	Timing	Diversity	Clarity
Brief description	How does the task align with learning outcomes and other requirements (such as graduate attributes)? (Use separate sheet for detailed evaluation.)	Is the task suitable in terms of its method, format, level, and weighting? (Use separate sheet for detailed evaluation.)	How is the timing of this task in terms of level of student learning, student workload, and feedback?	How does this task contribute to the diversity or otherwise of assessment methods for the course/ programme?	Is the task clear (not too ambiguous and not too detailed)?

Table D2: Worksheet for evaluating the method of assessment

Task	Type	Format	Mode	Difficulty	Weighting
Brief description of the task	Is the type of task (e.g., formative, diagnostic, summative) appropriate? Are changes required?	Is the format of the task (e.g., essay) appropriate to measure the outcomes? Are there better alternatives?	Is the mode of the task (e.g., in–class test) appropriate? Are there better alternatives?	Is the difficulty of the task appropriate in terms of skill level and complexity?	Is the task at an appropriate weighting to reflect its importance, contribution to learning outcomes, and student workload?

Table D3: Worksheet for detailed evaluation of assessment alignment with ILOs

Task	Weighting	Unit intended learning outcome	Course level or graduate learning outcomes assessed
Brief description of what students are to do	%	Which outcomes are assessed?	Which outcomes are assessed?

98   *Appendices*

Appendix E. **Evaluating criteria and standards (Chapter 4)**

Table E1: Worksheet for evaluating the quality of criteria and standards

Task	Alignment	Distinctness	Clarity and succinctness	Reasonableness	Level
Brief description of task	Do the criteria and standards link directly to the task and its requirements? What changes need to be made	Are the standards of achievement distinct and definite? What changes need to be made	Do the descriptors convey the meaning of each standard, clearly and succinctly? What changes need to be made	Are the marks at each standard reasonable for the effort and benefit? What changes need to be made	Are the standards too easy/trivial or impossible to achieve? What changes need to be made

Appendices 99

Appendix F. **Planning feedback (Chapter 5)**

This example planner shows how giving feedback to students can be scheduled at the point of unit design. It includes Hattie and Timperley's (2007) "feed up, feed back [sic] and feed forward" (p. 88). This planner has been devised for a face-to-face 20-point enabling unit. As such there are multiple smaller tasks, and formative feedback is essential.

Table F1: Feedback planner example

Week	Formal assessment event (due Monday)	Feed...	Method
1		Up	Overview of criteria and standards expected of the unit: In lecture
2			
3	5% discussion board post	Up	Analysis of 10% analysis rubric: Lecture and tutorial
4		Back and forward to next task	Individual: Rubric & document mark-up, written summative comment
			General: Summary in lecture
5			
6	10% analysis	Up	Overview of 20% essay rubric: Lecture
7		Up	Self- and peer-marking of draft 20% essay using rubric: Tutorial
8		Back and forward to next task	Individual: Rubric & document mark-up, written summative comment on each criterion and overall
			General: Summary in lecture
Break	20% essay		
Break			
9		Back and forward to next task	Individual: Rubric & document mark-up, written summative comment on each criterion and overall
			General: Dedicated lecture (2h)
		Up	Overview of 10% group presentation rubric: Lecture and tutorial
10			
11	10% group presentation	Back and forward in general	Group: Rubric mark-up, written comment on each criterion

100 *Appendices*

Week	Formal assessment event (due Monday)	Feed...	Method
12	15% individual report (based on group presentation)		
Study week			
Exam week 1		Back and forward in general	Individual: Rubric & document mark-up, written summative comment on each criterion and overall
Exam week 2			
Exam week 3	40% examination		

Appendices 101

Appendix G. Planning unit evaluation (Chapter 7)

This example planner shows how each of the sources of evaluation data (Brookfield 1998) can be applied strategically throughout a unit.

Table G1: Unit evaluation planner example

Data source	Timing	Type of data/tools	Reflection on data/purpose
Students	Weekly	Informal assessment of understanding through questioning and monitoring of student engagement;	How are students engaging with the unit material, assessments, etc.?
		Monitor discussion boards	Can I detect areas of difficulty or misunderstanding?
	After each assessment	Quality of student work; summary of student feedback given	Have the learning activities leading up to this assessment been successful? What areas of student work need my attention, and what learning activities can I change/ introduce?
			Does the assessment and/or rubric need alteration?
	Lecture 3	Student responses to key questions using Audience Response System (ARS), also known as clickers	How are students understanding this key area of difficulty? Do I need to change or add to the main learning activity?
	Week 4	Mid-semester Student Satisfaction survey	How are the students finding my teaching? What should I stop, start, or continue?
	Lecture 10	Student responses to key questions using ARS	How are students understanding this key area of difficulty? Do I need to change or add to the main learning activity?
	Post-unit	Formal student feedback on the unit	How did the students rate different aspects of the unit, and why?
Peers	Prior to unit	Peer review of assessment tasks and rubrics	How clearly have I articulated the tasks, criteria and standards? Do they need revision?
	Lecture 3	Peer observation	Is this lecture effective?
	Week 5	Review of Mid-semester Student Satisfaction survey	What advice does X have for me regarding my response to this survey?

102 *Appendices*

Data source	Timing	Type of data/tools	Reflection on data/purpose
Self	After each class or interaction	Notes of reflection: teaching and learning activities	What worked well, what didn't, what might I change in future: – Technically? – Operationally? – Philosophically?
	Post-unit	All data collected thus far, then reviewed by team	What is the implication of the data for: – ILO design? – Assessment design? – Rubric design? – Teaching & learning activity design?
Scholarly literature	Post-unit	Consult Teaching and Learning Centre	What has been done elsewhere to address …? What is the theoretical background for various approaches to unit design?

References

Brookfield, S. 1998, 'Critically reflective practice', *Journal of Continuing Education in the Health Professions*, vol. 18, no. 4, pp. 197–205.

Hattie, J. & Timperley, H. 2007, 'The power of feedback', *Review of Educational Research*, vol. 77, no. 1, pp. 81–112.

Index

Page numbers in **bold** indicate Tables.

action verbs **22**, **25**
active learning 78
affects, learning experiences 68–70
analysis, defined 74
analytical rubric 45, 46
Assessment 2020 (Boud & Associates) 29–30
assessment design: avoiding ambiguity 35; focus on student learning 32–37; functions of 28; goal of 29; integrity for 37–38; key features of 29; key principles for 30–32; learning outcomes and 39; summative tasks 31, 32–35
assessment literacy 37
assessment methods 30, **32–34**
assessment process: involving students in 2, 35, 56–57; stakeholders in 35–37, **36**; strategies for 38
assessments: alignment with ILOs 97; categories 30; characteristics of 29; criterion-referenced assessment 38; evaluating method of 96; evaluating suitability of tasks 96; focus on student learning 32–37; highest standard 49, **50**; internal consistency 32; next-to-highest standard 49, **50**; norm-referenced assessment 38; process of 28; reliability of 35, 43, 47–48; summative tasks 46; task outcomes 31; types of 32; validity in 31–32, 43; *see also* assessment design, rubrics
assessment workload 30
asynchronous learning activities 67, 78
Australian Qualifications Framework (AQF) 7, 15
authentic assessment tasks 35
authentic learning 29

backwards mapping 77
Benjamin Bloom and Associates 21
Biggs, John 18–20, 76
biological impacts of learning experiences 69–70
blind marking 38
Bloom's Taxonomy 21–23, 49, 71

cognition 68
cognitive processes: action verbs for **22**, **25**; categorising 21–22; Krathwohl's two-dimensional cognitive processes framework 22–24, **23**; learning outcomes 71; strategic rationale and 8, 26
coherent course design 2
communication skills 31
competence 38
constructive alignment 8, 20–21, 30, 76
construct validity 31–32
content validity 31
course, defined 1
course design, coherent *see* coherent course design, unit design
criterion-referenced assessment 38
criterion validity 31
critical thinking 71
curriculum alignment 8–9, 83
curriculum design *see* unit design
curriculum mapping 8

deep learning 71, **72–73**, 78
Delors, Jaques 14
descriptive feedback 61
Dewey, John 2, 84
diagnostic assessment 32

104 Index

dialogic feedback cycle 54 *see also* feedback
distinct descriptors 47–48
double marking 38

education and training 3
European Qualifications Framework (EQF) 15
evaluation 74
evaluative feedback 61
experiential learning 89
experimental design 45

feedback: analysing 58; development of 53; dialogic feedback cycle 54; draft submission 57; external sources 60; formative feedback 60–61; general feedback 59; individual feedback 58; individual reflections 60; internal sources 60; jig-saw 60; pair chatting 59; peer marking 57–58; personal feedback 58; post-task activities 58–60; pre-submission activities 55–58; quality of 60–61, 62; relevant 54; rubric deconstruction 55; rubrics and 42, 43; sample marking 55–56; self-marking 56; at self/personal level 61; seven principles of effective 53; student engagement 53, 54, 59–60; on student learning 32; task requirements aligned with 54; timeliness of 41, 54, 61–62; usefulness of 59
feedback planner 97, **98**
feed forward 42, 54, 57–58
feed up 42, 54, 55–58, 97
formative feedback 60–61
functionalism to education 2

general feedback 59
generic rubrics 45
grading 43, 46
graduate outcomes: measurement of 7; strategies for 7; work-readiness 13

Hattie, John 52
Higher Education Standards Framework 7
high-order thinking processes 68, 71–74
high-stakes learning activities 78
holistic rubrics 46
house-building analogy 8

indistinct descriptors 48
individual feedback 58
inference 74

inquiry-based learning 10
Intended Learning Outcomes (ILOs): acknowledging student's role in learning 16; assessment alignment of 97; assessment methods for **32–34**, 64; assessment task outcomes 31; defined 14; drafting of 18–21; example of 16–18, **19**; mapping process 20–21, 47; measurement of 15; objectively measurable 18; planning sheet 95; pre- and post-revisions **19**; retrofitting preferred assessment method to 32; unit designers' evaluation sheet 94; *see also* learning outcomes
internal consistency 8, 20, 32
internal feedback 60
International Commission on Education for the 21st Century report 14

jig-saw feedback 60

Krathwohl's two-dimensional cognitive processes framework 22–24, **23**

learner-centred education and training 3, 75
learner success 15
learning: assurance of 38; authentic 29; deep approach to 71, **72–73**; feedback on 32; issues and perspectives on **6**; off-campus 64; passive learning 71; problem-based approach 9–10; student achievements and 29; surface learning 71, **72–73**; UNESCO pillars of learning 14–15; *see also* learning activities, learning experiences, learning outcomes
learning activities: active learning 78; for active student participation 67–68; backwards mapping 77; characteristics of **79–80**; delivery of 66–67; demonstrating understanding 17; derived from learning outcomes 77; inference and 74; learning experiences vs. 66–67; low-stakes/high-stakes 78; as "out-of-class" 78; scheduled vs. unscheduled 66–67; synchronous vs. asynchronous 67
learning design: aligning with content, skills and knowledge 81; defined 64; documenting **77**
learning experiences: affects 68–70; alternatives to 65; characteristics of effective 77–78; cognitive 68;

Index 105

designing 64–66; design suggestions 78–81; higher education framework **65**; learning activities vs. 66–67; metacognitive strategies 76; modularising the unit 78; personalised learning 65–66; self-directed 66
learning outcomes: action verbs 21–25, **25**; assessment design and 39; characteristics of effective 16–17; cognitive process dimension 71; knowledge dimension 71; learning performance and 15; purpose of 14–15; qualification levels 15; student achievements 7, 25, 29; unit objectives vs. 16–17; word choice in writing 17; writing 16–18; *see also* Intended Learning Outcomes (ILOs)
learning resources 74
Learning to Teach in Higher Education (Ramsden) 75–76
low-order thinking processes 68
low-stakes learning activities 78

mapping process 47
mark allocation 43–44
marking guides 41, 55–57
Massively Open Online Courses (MOOCs) 3
mentor-mentee relationships 88
metacognition 42, 70, 76
motivations 88–89

norm-referenced assessment 38

objective test questionnaires 38
outcome-based education 13 *see also* learning outcomes

panel marking 38
passive learning 71
peer evaluation 87–88
peer marking 57–58
performance standards 45 *see also* student performance
personal feedback 58
personalised learning 65–66
practice-based learning 30
problem-based learning 9–10, 30

Race, P. 37
reflection 42, 60, 84, 89
"Reflex Arc" (Dewey) 2
rubrics: aligning with tasks 47; characteristics of 41–43; as clarification

of expectations 42; clarity and succinctness of 48; defined 40; defining student work quality and performance 41–42; design characteristics 41; development strategies 43–49, 53; distinct descriptors 47–48; evaluating new/existing 46–49; evaluative terms 44; as feed-forward mechanism 39; grading effectiveness and 43; grading reliability 46; as guide for teaching/learning process 42; marking guides 41; necessity of 40; reasonable criteria in 48–49; standards 44–45; steps for creating 49; structuring 43–45, **44**; students in development of 56–57; substantive conversation 57; types of 45–46; validity in 47; weighting of criterion 49; *see also* assessments

scheduled learning activities 66–67
self-checking 42
self-concept 69
self-efficacy 69
self-esteem 69
self-evaluation 70, 88–89
self-marking 56
SOLO (Structure of Observed Learning Outcome) Taxonomy **24**, 49
stakeholders 35–37, **36**
statements of knowledge 16
strategic rationale 7–10, **9**, 26, 87
student achievements 7, 25, 29 *see also* learning outcomes
student engagement 53, 54, 59–60, 75
student feedback *see* feedback
student judgement 42
student performance 6, 11, 18, 20, 45–46
student readiness 56
students as partners 85–87, **86**
substantive conversation 57
summative assessment tasks 31, 32–35, 46
surface learning 71, **72–73**
synchronous collaborative learning 67, 78
synchronous learning activities 67

Tang, Catherine 18–20
task requirements 54
task-specific rubric 45
taxonomies: action verbs **25**; Bloom's Taxonomy 21–23; SOLO (Structure of Observed Learning Outcome) Taxonomy 24
taxonomy of educational objectives 21

106 *Index*

teacher-centred education and training 3
teachers *see* unit designers
teaching, for successful learning 74–76
Teaching for Quality Learning at University
   (Biggs) 76
teaching peers 88
Tertiary Education Quality and Standards
   Agency (TEQSA) 7
thinking processes 68
transition pedagogy 37

UNESCO pillars of learning 14–15
unit design: administrative considerations
   6–7; analysing the context 3–4, 92–93;
   approach to 18–20; assessments of (*See*
   assessments); avoiding ambiguity 55;
   challenges for 5–7; coherence in 20;
   common course philosophy 5;
   consistency in 20; education funding
   and 6–7; factors influencing 3–4;
   historical perspectives 1–2;
   house-building analogy 8; inquiry-
   based approach 10; misconceptions 74;
   philosophical approaches to **4**; planning
   and development 1–2; problem-based
   approach 9–10; situational analysis for
   5; strategies for 7–10; teaching
   evaluations and 43; teaching
   perspectives in 10; *see also* unit
   designers, unit design evaluation
unit designers: effectiveness of feedback
   53; ILO checker 94; motivations
   88–89; reflective practice 85; rubrics
   and 47; student feedback 86–87;
   working in course framework 6
unit design evaluation: checklist 90;
   criteria for **84**; improving quality 83;
   peer feedback 87–88; reflective practice
   84–85; students as partners in 85–87;
   systematic review 83
unit evaluation planner 99, **99–100**
unit performance 83
units of study, defined 1
university education: challenges for 1–2;
   funding for design resources 6–7; value
   of 1
unscheduled learning activities 66–67

visualisation 70

whole of course approach *see* coherent
   course design